PEOPLE OF THE WORD

A Synopsis of Slovak History

Thomas Klimek Ward

PEOPLE OF THE WORD

A Synopsis of Slovak History

MATICA SLOVENSKÁ 2000

The author would like to express his gratitude to the Matica Slovenská Foundation for its financial support of this volume.

Thomas Klimek Ward

PEOPLE OF THE WORD
A Synopsis of Slovak History

Published by:
Vydavateľstvo Matice slovenskej
Mudroňova 1
036 52 Martin
Slovakia
Tel. (+421842), 422 06 92, Fax: (+421842) 413 45 35

Frontispiece – *Rastislav, Prince of the Slovaks, welcomes Constantine-Cyril, Methodius and the emissaries of the Byzantine Emperor Michael III to his court.*
Tapestry entitled, *The Byzantine Mission in Great Moravia* by Mikuláš Klimčák.
Courtesy of the artist

Editor: Mgr. Juliana Krébesová
English text read by: PhDr. Jana Stachová
Graphic design: Igor Štrbík

Text © Thomas Klimek Ward, 2000
© 2000 Matica Slovenská

Printed by Neografia a.s., Martin

First Edition, 2000

All rights reserved. No part jof this book may be used or reproduced in any manner whatsoever without written permission.

ISBN 80–7090–602–2

DEDICATION

To
my Mother,
Helen Veronica Klimek Ward
and
my Father,
Thomas James Ward
and
To All the Sons and Daughters
of the
Slovak Nation
past, present and future...
so that their story
will always be remembered!

Contents

Dedication		5
Foreword		8
Preface		9
Acknowledgements		10
Introduction		13
Chapter One	Prelude – Out of the Mists of Time	17
Chapter Two	The Seventh through the Ninth Centuries	26
Chapter Three	The Tenth through the Fifteenth Centuries	55
Chapter Four	The Sixteenth through the Eighteenth Centuries	65
Chapter Five	The Nineteenth Century	81
Chapter Six	The Twentieth Century – The End and The Beginning	93
Chronology of Historical Events		105
List of Rulers of Slovakia		108
Bibliography		111
Glossary		115
Picture Credits		119
Index		121

Foreword

This book is a labor of love and enthusiasm in which Thomas Klimek Ward celebrates his Slovak heritage. As an adult, Tom learned to speak, read and write Slovak, the language of his ancestors, the knowledge of which, together with the education gained as an experienced traveller, greatly assisted him in this endeavor. He is a strong promoter of Slovak culture and heritage. In 1995, Tom was appointed by the Slovak Government as the first Honorary Consul of the Slovak Republic in Chicago. His desire to introduce Slovakia to a wider audience has led him to undertake its story.

Although he holds a Bachelor's Degree in History from the University of Illinois at Chicago, Tom's work is not intended to be an academic study, but rather a summation and synthesis of his own study of the Slovak past. Tom has taken what he has found to be absorbing moments of Slovak history and woven them into a narrative which can be appreciated by a general readership. It is his hope that this treatise will lead its readers to come to an appreciation of the struggle of peoples and cultures for self-fulfillment, to search deeper into their own roots and to embark, as he did, on a journey of discovery.

Susan Mikula, Ph.D.
Professor of History
Benedictine University
Lisle, Illinois

Preface

The life of this volume can be attributed to the continual, but always gracious, prodding requests of a dear friend for a series of articles on Slovak history. Its intent is to serve as an introduction and overview of the history of the Slovak nation; it is not designed to be an in depth study of that history.

Hopefully, while whetting the appetite of its readers, it will enkindle in them a desire to learn more about the Slovak nation and Slovakia, the country which is the actual geographic „Heart of Europe", and to encourage them to peruse the great store of Slovak historical and cultural works available outside the realm of this modest work.

A great many individuals contributed in a variety of ways to the production of this book; to all of them I give my sincere and heartfelt thanks. I would be remiss, however, if I did not mention some of them: Ilonka Martinka Torres, without whose encouragement and prodding, this book would probably never have been written; Rosemary Macko Wisnosky for her invaluable insights and knowledge of linguistics and grammar; Susan Mikula, PhD. for her perceptive and objective commentaries, expertise and review of the contents; Roman Hudec and Viliam Pačes for their help in translating Slovak sources and Dr. František Vnuk for reviewing the manuscript for technical accuracy. I also extend a very special thank you to my parents and my family and to all the unnamed friends for their tremendous support and help.

Thomas Klimek Ward
July 5, 2000

Acknowledgements

A special thank you is also merited by the following individuals and organizations who kindly assisted with the diverse aspects and in various stages of this book's preparation:
Mr. Ricardo Belluti, B. N. Marconi Arte Grafiche, Genoa, Italy
Rev. Fr. Leonard Boyle, O.P., Irish Dominican Fathers, Basilica of St. Clement and the Vatican Library, Rome, Italy
Ing. Ján Brezovský, Mayor of the City of Hlohovec, Slovakia
Rev. Fr. Giuseppe Casetta, O.S.B., Vallombrosian Benedictine Monks, Rector, Basilica of St. Praxedes, Rome, Italy
Mrs. Terézia Jahelková-Čechová, Hlohovec, Slovakia
Ing. Vladimír Čierny, Remium Productions, Pezinok, Slovakia
Consul General Pasquale D'Avino, Consulate General of Italy in Chicago, Illinois, U.S.A.
Rev. Fr. Michael Dunleavy, O.P., Rector, Basilica of St. Clement, Rome
Mr. Evan Evangelidis, Archivist, Greek Orthodox Archdiocese of America, New York, New York, U.S.A.
Mr. Paul Evans, Art Resource, New York, New York, U.S.A.
Mrs. Valéria Farkašová, Topoľčany, Slovakia
Ms. Helen Fedor, Library of Congress, Washington, D. C., U.S.A.
Mr. Karol Felix, Nitra, Slovakia
First Catholic Slovak Ladies Association, Beachwood, Ohio, U.S.A.
First Catholic Slovak Union, Independence, Ohio, U.S.A.
Ing. Agáta Palenčarová-Fogel, Fremont, California, U.S.A.
Ing. Ľubomír Fraňo, Nitra, Slovakia
Dr. Ivona Fraňová, Nitra Information System Office, Nitra, Slovakia
Dr. Paul V. Gallo, D.D.S., Naperville, Illinois, U.S.A.

Mrs. Barbora Jahelková-Gerová, Hlohovec, Slovakia
Mr. Nunzio Grieco, Italian National Tourist Office, Chicago, Illlinois, U.S.A.
Mrs. Oľga Grünnerová, Bratislava, Slovakia
Mgr. Štefan Haviar, Matica slovenská, Martin, Slovakia
Mr. Constantine Hliavoris, Greek National Tourist Organization, New York, New York, U.S.A.
Mr. Pavol Holeštiak, Vzlet Publications, Čadca, Slovakia
Mr. Pavel Jahelka and Mrs. Jozefína Jahelková, Hlohovec, Slovakia
Mr. Michal Jamrich and Mrs. Elena Jamrichová, Hlohovec, Slovakia
Dr. Dušan Karaska, Director, Orava Museum, Dolný Kubín, Slovakia
Mr. Mikuláš Klimčák, Bratislava, Slovakia
Prof. Martha Mistina Kona, Wilmette, Illinois, U.S.A.
Ing. Jozef Korec, Office of the Mayor, Nitra, Slovakia
Mgr. Juliana Krébesová, Matica slovenská, Martin, Slovakia
JUDr. Jozef Kudla, City Manager, City of Hlohovec, Slovakia
Ladies Pennsylvania Slovak Catholic Union, Wilkes-Barre, Pennsylvania, U.S.A.
Rt. Rev. Msgr. D. J. David Lewis, Rector, College of Santa Maria Magggiore, Rome, Italy
Mr. Leonidas Marinakos, Honorary Cultural Attaché, Consulate General of Greece in Chicago, Illinois, U.S.A.
Ing. Jozef Markuš, DrSc., Chairman, Matica slovenská, Bratislava, Slovakia
Ing. Juraj Moravčik, Former Deputy Mayor of the City of Nitra, Slovakia
Ms. Pavlína Moravčiková, Bratislava, Slovakia
Ms. Susan Bolsom-Morris, Calmann & King, London, England
Mgr. Stanislav Muntág, Matica slovenská, Martin, Slovakia
Mrs. Marta Novotná, Nitra, Slovakia
Rt. Rev. Msgr. František Novajovský, Rector, Pontifical Slovak College of Saints Cyril and Methodius, Rome, Italy
Mr. Richard A. O'Sullivan, Morris, Illinois, U.S.A.
Mgr. Ivan Pastorek, Director, Vlastivedné Múzeum and Archives, Hlohovec, Slovakia
Mgr. Ivan Pavlisko, Ružomberok, Slovakia
Mrs. Helena Pekarovičová, Director, Municipal Library, Hlohovec, Slovakia

Rt. Rev. Msgr. Ján Pristáč, Rector, Seminary of Saints Cyril and Methodius, Bratislava, Slovakia

Mr. Alexander Psica, Vlastivedné Múzeum and Archives, Hlohovec, Slovakia

Mr. Fulvio Rocco, Italian General Directorate Service of Cults, Rome, Italy

Slovak Catholic Sokol, Passaic, New Jersey, U.S.A.

Mgr. Milan Straka, Matica slovenská, Martin, Slovakia

Mgr. Igor Štrbík, Matica slovenská, Martin, Slovakia

Consul Maria Theodorou, Consulate General of Greece in Chicago, Illinois, U.S.A.

Prof. Philip Tuhy and Mrs. Trude Check Tuhy, Wilkes-Barre, Pennsylvania, U.S.A.

Ing. Arch. Dr. Andrea Urlandová, Bratislava, Slovakia

JUDr. Štefan Valent, Nitra, Slovakia

JUDr. Dagmar Veliká, Bratislava, Slovakia

Ing. Lydia Vojtaššáková, Habovka, Slovakia

Ing. Vladimír Žuffa, Zuberec, Slovakia

And to my maternal grandparents, *Magdaléna Jahelková Klimeková* and *Štefan Alojz Klimek*, who instilled in me, by song, word and tradition, a special love for the land of my ancestors.

Introduction

Slovakia, and the "Slovak World," which we understand to be those areas which are inhabited by Slovaks and their descendants throughout the world, jointly represent a complicated, multi-dimensional and varied reality of a large network of connections and relationships. Slovak history is a constant. It can be researched either from the inside or the outside, from the center or the periphery or from an antagonistic or sympathetic outlook. In the world at large I believe that there is, unfortunately, an insufficient knowledge of Slovak history and that this history should be studied from various points of view.

People of the Word: A Synopsis of Slovak History deals with Slovak history from the point of view of the North American continent. It is an American-Slovak view as well as a global one, but an outlook that is also characteristically Slovak. At the same time it is the viewpoint of a unique personality discovering Slovakia and the Slovak nation for himself and in behalf of others, the viewpoint of an individual whose own personal history is an interesting part of the mosaic of both Slovak and international multi-cultural history.

Thomas Klimek Ward's approach to Slovak history evolves from a different perspective than that of those of us who live in Slovakia. I believe his book will be a most enlightening and appealing source of information to a worldwide English speaking public, who, for the most part, know very little about Slovakia or the Slovak people. And finally, the Slovak historical awareness of those Slovaks who have lived abroad in Slovak and non-Slovak communities for two, three, four and sometimes even five generations is largely limited and, therefore, an up-to-date account of the history of Slovakia is truly desirable. In other words, this book provides much fundamental and essential information about Slovak history and promulgates that history as it opens the door to a deeper knowledge and understanding of Slovakia and the Slovaks. Through its publication and dissemination, this book also contributes to the fulfillment one of the main objectives of the Matica Slovenská as it enters the twenty-first century.

    I would like to thank the Matica Slovenská and, in particular, the author, Thomas Klimek Ward, the Honorable Consul of the Slovak Republic in Illinois, for his great effort and devotion to the writing of this book as well as for his ardent and generous support of the Matica Slovenská.

Jozef Markus
Chair of Matica Slovenska

Slovakia

Slovakia in Europe

CHAPTER ONE

Prelude – Out of the Mists of Time

The period covering the years from 300 B.C. to 600 A.D. is usually referred to as the Great Movement or Migration of the Nations. It was a time of upheaval during which waves of people poured out of central Asia eastward, southward and, in the case of the Indo-Europeans, westward. They included, among others, Celts, Goths, Vandals, Visigoths and Slavs.

In regard to the original homeland of the ancestors of the proto-Slovaks, various writers have ascribed it to India, to central Asia, to present day western Ukraine and it has even been argued that they are indigenous to central Europe itself. Wherever that origin might lay, within a hundred years of the death of the Pannonian-born western Roman emperor, Valentinian I in 375 A. D. and the collapse of the *Limes Romanus,* the Roman frontier system, the settlements of the proto-Slovaks were already firmly established on the present day territory of Slovakia. And the irreversible process of development from proto-Slav to Early Slav to proto-Slovak to Old Slovak had already commenced. By the ninth century the settlements of the Old Slovaks extended from west of the Morava River to east of the Tisa River, and from south of the Danube to the peaks of the High Tatra mountains in the north.

To construct the early history of the Slovak people is to indeed reach back into the mists of time. The early Slavic/proto-Slovak ancestors of the Slovaks were known and written about by a variety of Greek, Roman, Goth and Byzantine authors, including the historians Cassius Dio, Herodotus,

Jordanes, Ammianus Marcellinus, Velleius Paterculus, Pliny the Elder, Procopius, Claudius Ptolemy, Tacitus and Theophylactus. These writers, for the most part, used the designation Slavs, or a closely related similar term when referencing them, but some of them also referred to them by the name Venedae or Wends, as did some of the Germanic peoples.

Despite the fact that knowledge of the origins and early history of the Slovaks is so hazy, we still have enough information to give us a cursory glimpse into some of their pre-Christian beliefs and ways of life. It would appear that the pagan Slovaks, for the most part, fashioned their gods and goddesses from the forces of nature that played such a major role in their daily lives. To these deities they offered their invocations and supplications and, to them, they attributed the blessings and misfortunes that filled their existence.

At the summit of that pantheon of numerous gods and goddesses loomed their chief or supreme being *Praboh*, considered the father god or great god. Below *Praboh, Bielboh*, the white god and *Čiernoboh*, the dark or black god held sway, in what can be termed pagan Slovak personifications of a basic belief in a dualistic, compartmentalized ordering of nature; good and evil, creation and destruction, life and death, white and black. The sun god, or perhaps more accurately the sky god, *Svaroh* was invoked under several different appellations, including the names *Dažboh, Svetovid* and *Radhosť*. These descriptive designations for the sky/sun god seemed to have been used to distinguish him under the guise of his various other aspects and attributes, that is, as *Dažboh*, the god of rain/bounty, *Svetovid*, the god of light/goodness, and *Radhosť*, the benevolent protector god of wisdom. Idols of a Slavic divinity with three and even four heads have been unearthed; and these figures of „*triglav/trihlav*", i.e., the „triune"[1] or „three headed" one, may have represented different aspects or seasonal counterparts of the same divinity. His son, the god of fire was called, appropriately enough, *Svarožič*, that is, the Son of Brightness. Among the most feared and dreaded of the ancient pagan Slovak gods, however, was *Parom*,[2] the god of thunder and lightning, who, when his anger was kindled, or perhaps just for mere sport, sent forth his thunderbolts to smote both the earth and its occupants. Inhabiting the realm of darkness as well were sundry demons, crones, wizards, witches and *Morena*, the goddess of

---

[1] It is interesting to theorize that one of the reasons why the Slavs made a fairly rapid transition from paganism to Christianity, once it was introduced among them, may have been because of a predilection for a triune or trinitarian god.

[2] After a trip to Slovakia during the summer of 1968, I remember inquiring about a shepherd we had met, and with whom we had shared *bryndza* (a famous Slovak cheese made from sheep's milk) and *žinčica* (the boiled sweet whey) at an authentic Slovak *salaš* (sheep farm) in the Low Tatra mountain region. I was informed that he had later been struck and killed by lightning. The words, in Slovak, used to describe his death were „*Parom ho trafil*/Parom struck him down." Likewise, in another discussion with Slovak-born friends living in the United States, from the areas of both Bratislava and Košice, they also acknowledged familiarity with the same term, „*Parom ho trafil*", but as an archaic form of saying someone had died of a stroke. Other examples of such phrases exist in daily Slovak lingual usage, although they are fast fading in our modern world. They are, however, prime examples of the enduring ancient collective memories of a nation's past, even when the true meanings have sometimes been lost or obscured over the course of centuries.

death. The priests and priestesses serving the denizens of the dark forces, the so-called *čiernobožstva*, dressed in garments of black; for which reason they were referred to as the *čiernokňažníctvo*, i.e., the black priesthood.

Divinities who looked more favorably on the ancient Slovaks were: *Lada*, the goddess of beauty and love; *Vesna*, the goddess of Spring; and the agricultural goddesses, *Živa* and *Úroda*, which may or may not have been two aspects of the same goddess. There were also numerous other minor divinities residing in the sphere of the Slovak supernatural including *Zmok*, who was affiliated with good luck, *Znachor* with knowledge and *Škriatok*, an impish deity, who watched over the household. The priestly caste that tended to the worship of the *bielobožstvá* (the forces of light) wore vestments of white and thus were called the *bielokňazi* or white priests. Within the realm of the paranormal also fell those elements who were *čiernokňažníci* (sorcerers), *vedomkyne* (seeresses), *čarodejníci* (magicians) and *veštice* (fortune-tellers). Prophets and seeresses claimed the power to foresee the future and likewise practiced the arts of healing. Sorcerers and magicians claimed an assortment of mystical powers including the ability to change humans into animals or into other forms. Other members of that spirit world included a variety of water nymphs, such as the *víly* (singular: *víla*), who inhabited certain brooks and creeks and who were both kind and nasty. There were also, the beautiful but treacherous *rusalky* (singular: *rusalka*), who likewise made their abode in rivers and streams and attempted to seduce all unwary passersby to a watery grave in their clammy domains.

The goddess Morena, who personified both death and winter, was among the most dreaded and feared of the ancient Slovak pagan gods and goddesses. Painting by Ivan Pavlisko

Additional spirit inhabitants included the *lesné panny* (singular: *lesná panna*), the forest maidens, who resided in the great dense, primeval forests of Slovakia. Further tenants of that mythical world of magic and lore consisted of *vlkodlaci* (werewolves), *pikulíci* (gnomes), *besovia* (evil spirits), *piadimužíci* (dwarfs), *ďasovia* (devil spirits), *loktibrady* (trolls) and *vodníci* (water spirits).

The most common place of worship for the pagan Slovaks seems to have been in consecrated groves, where they raised stone or wooden images of their deities and performed

Vesna, the Old Slovak pagan goddess of spring, evoked images of beauty and the stirrings of new life in her adherents. Painting by Ivan Pavlisko

The main attributes of Parom, worshipped by the ancient pagan Slovaks as their god of war, were thunder and lightning. Painting by Ivan Pavlisko

their sacrificial rites. Attending to the worship of the gods was a special class of sacrificial priests called *žreci* (singular: *žrec*). Sacrificial offerings, called *žertva*, were almost invariably in the form of grains, plants or animals. Rarely was human sacrifice practiced and that customarily only in wartime, with the victim usually being one of the enemy.[3] Winter heralded the arrival of the goddess of winter and death, *Morena*, while spring was celebrated as the joyous return of the goddess, *Vesna*. The summer solstice, referred to by the various terms *Turíce*, *Letnice* and *Rusadlá*, was celebrated as the resurgence of the sun god, *Svaroh*, while the winter solstice, called the feast of *koleda* commemorated *Svetovid's* defeat of *Čiernoboh*, the victory of light over darkness.

Offerings were made to the dead, as well as to the gods and goddesses. In cases of persons of rank, such as a *knieža* (prince), *vojvoda* (duke) or *náčelník* (chieftain), the body might be buried in a specially raised earthwork mound or a cairn called a *mohyla*, so that the memory of the departed person would be preserved for future generations. In pagan Slovak society, the deceased's wife, or a maiden, might also be sacrificed, in order to accompany him on his journey to the other world. Inside these tombs various artifacts, utensils, jewelry and weapons were also buried with the dead.

Cremation, however, was the usual form of corporal disposal, with the remains of the deceased then being placed in a clay pot-like burial urn called a *popolnica*, which was then buried in a mortuary. The mortuaries that have been unearthed so far have usually been found close to brooks and streams, located near ancient Slovak citadels or village areas. Several of these popolnica-type urns have been discovered and excavated in the environs of a number of Slovak towns such as Hlohovec and Nitra and in various other Slovak locales including Turiec, Novohrad, Liptov, Skalica and Devínska Nová Ves to mention only a few.

First in a series of intaglios, entitled Dcéra Slávy – Daughter of Glory by Karol Felix, embodying the artist's conception of the spirit of Slovakia's Great Moravian Empire. Courtesy of the artist

---

[3] Human sacrifice was indigenous not only to the pagan Slavs, but to the pagan Celts, Germans, Greeks, Romans, etc.

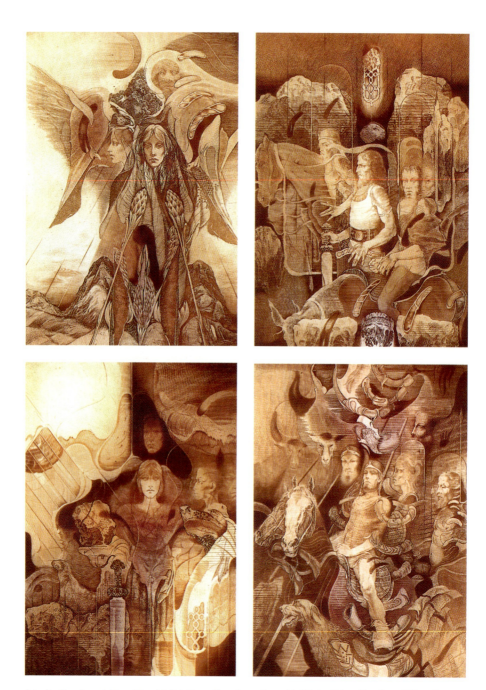

Intaglios Two through Five of Karol Felix's Great Moravian series entitled Dcéra Slávy – Daughter of Glory. Courtesy of the artist

During the eighth and ninth centuries, the Old Slovaks began to raise a number of large fortified defense structures and castles. Besides the well-known Slovak Great Moravian sites of Devín, Bratislava and Nitra, recorded by the Frankish chroniclers in their annals, mention is also made of the citadel of Hlohovec, though where it stood, in relation to present day Hlohovec, is subject to question. Theoretically, two sites lend themselves as excellent possibilities. These are the location where the present castle stands overlooking the Váh River, which according to one of the castle's chatelaines, also harbored Roman

Devín Castle was strategically constructed above the confluence of the Danube and Morava rivers. Settlement of the area dates back to 5000 B.C. It was also home to the Celts and the Romans, and a major crossroads on the Amber Route, before becoming one of the major Great Moravian centers during the reigns of Rastislav and Svätopluk I. Picture courtesy of the Matica Slovenská

ruins within its walls and is the presumed site where once stood the ancient Roman castellum, or citadel, of Elenthereopolis;[4] or on the main square where today stands the Roman Catholic Church of Saint Michael the Archangel, originally built in the thirteenth century, most probably on the site of an earlier church and, in whose vicinity gravesites from the Great Moravian era have been excavated.

---

[4] On a visit to Hlohovec during the latter part of October 1965, I was shown the purported site of Elenthereopolis, by my grandmother's brother, Pavel Jahelka of Hlohovec. If memory serves me correctly, it was in the very near vicinity of present day Hlohovec Castle.

The Nitra Castle-Cathedral Complex, in the city of Nitra, renowned as the Mother of Slovak cities. Nitra was the premier Great Moravian center in Slovakia and the capital of Prince Pribina's domains, as well as the site of the first Christian church in Slovakia. Settlement in the area goes back 30,000 years. Photograph courtesy of the Nitra Information System Office

The Renaissance Maiden's Tower of Devín Castle became the setting of numerous Slovak legends. Photograph courtesy of the Matica Slovenská, from: Kultúrne dedičstvo Slovenska

Centers of the Great Moravian period, as well as other early Slovak sites likewise were situated at Šulekovo and Siladice in the vicinity of Hlohovec, Čierne Kľačany, Veľká Mača, Skalica, Majcichov near Trnava, Pobedim, Bíňa, Ducové, Zemplín, Trniny, Istebné-Hrádok and Ostrá Skala by Vyšný Kubín in Orava, Spišské Tomášovce, Hradec-Prievidza, Divinka-Žilina and Blatnohrad and Vyšehrad[5] (the latter two, located in what is today Hungary), to mention only a few localities.

Bratislava Castle rises majestically high above the River Danube and Slovakia's capital city, which bears the same name. Settlement on the castle mount dates back to 2500 B.C. Earlier Celtic and Roman settlements in the area antedate the arrival of the Old Slovaks who established a major center here. Picture courtesy of the Matica Slovenská

The shared traditions, beliefs and culture of the Old Slovaks and their fellow Slavs, which they had held in common since time immemorial, began to diverge in the eighth and ninth centuries. Thus the foundations were laid for the establishment of each of their distinct histories and the beginnings of individual cultures.

---

[5] Blatnohrad is today known as Zalavár, while Vyšehrad is still known by its Old Slovak name of Vyšegrad.

CHAPTER TWO

The Seventh through the Ninth Centuries

Whether under their ancient name of „the *Slovieni*" or its modern equivalent, „the *Slováci*," i.e. the Slovaks,[6] the defining name of the people of the Slovak nation has retained its meaning „*People of the Word*". Linguists trace its purport to the Slovak term, „*Slovo*" that is „The Word," and apply its origin to the Slavonic mother tongue that was mutually intelligible to, and the common language of, the early Slavs. History records that the celebrated priest Constantine the Philosopher,[7] after having created an alphabet, for the Old Slovaks, chose first to translate, into the Slavonic idiom of our ancestors, the Gospel of St. John. The Old Slavonic/Old Slovak gospel began, „*Iskoni bie Slovo...*" which is rendered in modern Slovak as „*Na počiatku bolo Slovo a Slovo bolo u Boha a Boh bol Slovo... In the beginning was the Word, and the Word was with God, and the Word was God.*" If in fact that was the case, then indeed, nothing else could have been more appropriate for a nation who referred to itself as the *People of*

---

[6] The term *Slověne* is used in some works for the immediate ancestors of the present day Slovaks. It should be noted that the term is confusing as it can also, in English, specifically mean a Slovenian, one of the South Slav nations. However, it must be stated that the word *Slověne*, written as such is a precursor for the word *Sloviene* and all related terms, which is the grammatically correct Slovak term. Other examples being the Slovak noun – *slovienčina* and the Slovak adjectives – *sloviensky, slovienska*, etc. that specifically denote the Old Slavonic/Old Slovak language and the terms Old Slavonic/Old Slovak respectively in the Slovak language.

[7] Constantine would only take the religious name of Cyril, when he became a monk, some months prior to his death.

the Word, to have as the first piece of writing in their literature, those words of Holy Writ that commence the Gospel of St. John the Evangelist, celebrating the *Logos*, the One Who is... the Word.

By the fifth century A.D., the Slav tribes who were to become the Slovak nation were already well-established between the Carpathian Mountains and the Danube River as well as along the banks of the rivers Nitra, Váh, Hron and Morava, in the territory known today as Slovakia (Slovensko) and Moravian Slovakia (Moravské Slovácko) and which comprised the nucleus of what is called the Great Moravian Empire. Organized into tribal structures, they lacked at this point, a unifying leadership and soon came under the dominion of the warlike Avars, a Mongolian horde, which had swept into the Danubian basin, from the steppes of Asia.

In the wake of the despoliation of their lands by the Avars and their khagan, Bajan, the Slovaks, under the leadership of a Frankish merchant named Samo, rose in rebellion and drove out the Avars in 623 A.D. Samo then proceeded to lay the foundation of the first unified and organized Slovak community referred to by historians as „Samo's Empire". Defending his new state, Prince Samo defeated King Dagobert and his army of Franks in 631 at the Castle of Vosgate.[8] The success of Samo's enterprise can be attested to by the fact that his empire endured for thirty-five years, until his death in 658. Unfortunately,

Prince Samo (circa 600 – 658), first recorded ruler of the Slovieni on the territory of Slovakia. Painting by Ivan Pavlisko

as with a number of empire-builders who died without able successors, the union Prince Samo had brought about also disintegrated upon his death. Once again besieged and overrun by the Avars, Samo's empire disappeared into the pages of history along with the Avars who were decisively defeated by the forces of Charlemagne in 799.

---

[8] Although the precise location of Vosgate Castle, i. e., Vogastisburg is unknown, one view presented is that it was either at Bratislava or at Devín, See Dominic Hudec, *Veľký omyl, Veľká Morava* (Martin: Matica Slovenská, 1994), pp. 41 – 43. Another argument is made for its location at Trenčín, Slovakia on the basis of Trenčín's Old Frankish name of Vogburg which was already known in 179 A. D. by the Roman appellation, Laugaricio. See Tomáš J. Veteška, *Veľkoslovenská ríša* (Hamilton: Zahraničná Matica Slovenská, 1987), pp. 29 – 30.

Knieža Pribina of Nitra, together with his wife, young son Koceľ and courtiers, receive the blessing of Archbishop Adalram of Salzburg in 828 A. D., as he consecrates the first Christian church in Pribina's domains. The edifice built by Prince Pribina, in Nitra, holds the distinction of being the first Christian church to be built in the lands of the Slavs. Painting by Maximilián Schurmann. Courtesy of JUDr. Štefan Valent. Photograph by Marta Novotná

Statue of Prince Pribina (circa 800 – 861) by Tibor Bártfay on Pribinovo námestie (Pribina Square) in Nitra. Photograph courtesy of the Nitra Information System Office

Faced with the power and influence of the rising Frankish and Bavarian kingdoms in their immediate environs, the importance of a unified commonwealth was not lost on the fledgling Slovak noble class that was beginning to arise and assert itself in the Principality of Nitra, located in western Slovakia.

Hoping to procure some of the benefits he perceived in those realms, Pribina, the Prince of Nitra, fostered the introduction of Christianity and the building of ecclesiastical structures in his lands. To him is attributed the distinct honor, in the year 828, of erecting the first Christian church, not only in Slovakia, but in all of Central Europe. Tradition had named the church he founded as that of the Roman Catholic Church of Saint Emeram, which is still functioning today, and is part of the Cathedral complex of Nitra; but it is now generally thought that Pribina's church was the Church of St. Martin,[9] which stood on Mount St. Martin in Nitra. Desiring to reap the benefits of education as well as to embellish his capital, Pribina, it is believed, also founded the Monastery of St. Hippolytus on the slopes of Mount Zobor. Sadly, the original monastery today lies in ruins, but its remains can still be viewed in the mountains surrounding the city of Nitra.

Ruins of the Monastery of St. Hippolytus on Mt. Zobor in Nitra. Originally established as a Benedictine foundation, it was later home to the Camaldolese Monks, whose rule combined both cenobitic and eremitical elements in their way of life. Photograph courtesy of the Nitra Information System Office

A rival of Pribina's, Mojmír of Moravian Slovakia,[10] had, in the meantime, cast an envious eye on the rising star of the House of Pribina and was determined to wrest control of the Principality of Nitra. Historically it would appear, however, that Mojmír won the battle and lost the war. For although he took the coveted prize of Nitra about 833 his subjects were soon raising arms against him in rebellion.

---

[9] Michal Lacko, and others present the view that the church founded by Prince Pribina was not that of the existing Church of St. Emeram, but that of the Church of Saint Martin which stood on Mount St. Martin under Mt. Zobor in Nitra. See Michael Lacko, „Great Moravia in the Light of Recent Research 1945 – 1975" in Joseph M. Kirschbaum (et al.) ed., *Slovak Culture Through the Centuries,* p. 78. John Rekem, *Zobor: The Mount and The Monastery* (Hamilton: Slovak Publishing, 1969), pp. 20 – 22.

[10] A clarification is needed here, as the term *Moravian* itself did not exist at this time, as a descriptive term for themselves

The Greek city of Thessalonika was the birthplace of Constantine-Cyril and Methodius. Founded in 315 B.C. by Cassander, it was named for his wife Thessaloniki, the step-sister of Alexander the Great. The first and second epistles of St. Paul to the Thessalonians were addressed to the city's early Christian converts and written about 50 A.D. They are believed to be the very first of the Pauline letters. Photograph courtesy of the Greek National Tourist Office, New York

The Basilica of St. George in Thessaloniki, Greece. Built circa 300 A.D., it was originally a part of the imperial palace of the Roman emperor Galerius. In the fifth century it was converted for use as a Christian church and dedicated to St. George the Megalomartyr, who died about 303 A.D. Photograph courtesy of the Greek National Tourist Office, New York

CHAPTER TWO / THE SEVENTH THROUGH THE NINTH CENTURIES

After the Treaty of Verdun in 843, his rule and military strength greatly diminished, and within three years the armies of Louis the German repaid him with the same coin he had given to Prince Pribina. Pribina, on the other hand, had been welcomed at the court of Count Rathbod of the Eastern Mark, was baptized into the Catholic faith, received with honor by King Louis

Detail of a bas relief section on the early fourth century Arch of Galerius in the center of Thessalonika, depicting episodes from the emperor's war against the Persians. Photograph courtesy of the Greek National Tourist Office, New York

and, in 847 established a new principality at Blatnohrad[11] (present day Zalavár, Hungary) on the banks of Lake Balaton in Pannonia.

---

by the then Slavic inhabitants of what is now called *Moravské Slovácko*. Frankish chroniclers were apparently the first to use a form of the term „Moravian" in the 800s, to describe the *Slovieni* in some of their annals. The term may have come from the fact that one of the greatest Slovieni fortress-castles was at Devín, in Slovakia, above the confluence of the Danube and Morava rivers. Also, it was not until, the Byzantine emperor, Constantine VII Porphyrogenitus (912 – 959) first used the term Great Moravia to describe the area of Slovakia and Moravské Slovácko in his writings that the term was used as nomenclature for the empire of the Slovieni. Prince Rastislav is referred to in the *Život Metoda* (The Life of Methodius), written in Old Slavonic and attributed to Methodius' protegé, the Slovak saint, Gorazd, as „*Rastislav, knieža slovienske,*" i. e., Rastislav, Prince of the Slovieni. Also, in his remarks to the Emperor Michael III, Rastislav is quoted as referring to himself and his people as „*my Slovieni* (We, the Slovieni)." See *Život Metoda*, Chapter 5, Peter Ratkoš, p. 69. No mention is made at all of the word Moravian. Their own term for themselves was thus the *Slovieni*, from which today's term, the Slovaks, is obviously derived. Those *Slovieni* living in what is present day *Moravské Slovácko* thus received a new foreign name for themselves, that of Moravian, in place of their own self-styled name of Slovieni, from foreigners. This name was perpetuated in Byzantine and Latin writings, until it eventually became even their own name for themselves. The Slovieni of Slovensko/Slovakia proper are, of course, the Slovaks.

[11] Pribina ruled at Blatnohrad until his death sometime about the beginning of the year 861, when he was succeeded by his son, Prince Koceľ.

The magnificent Basilica of Hagia Sophia built by the Emperor Justinian I (527 – 565) in Constantinople. Dedicated to the Holy Wisdom of the Logos, the Word, it was constructed in just five years and consecrated on Christmas Day in 537 A.D. In its day it was the largest and most magnificent Christian ecclesiastical structure the world had ever seen. Adjoining the Great Church stood the Patriarchal Palace and Library where Constantine the Philospher served as chartophylax. Photograph by Vanni

View of the nave of Justinian's Megalo Ecclesia from the imperial gallery reserved for the Byzantine Empress and her entourage. The emperor lavishly decorated the Great Church's interior with gold, silver, precious gems, mosaics and an array of marble from Europe, Asia and Africa. Photograph by Werner Forman

By the year 846 the Prince of Nitra was Rastislav, who ruled over the combined Nitrian and Moravian-Slovak lands. In 855, Louis the German unsuccessfully made war on Rastislav, the outcome of which was Louis' courtship of a Bulgar alliance. Anticipating the dangers of a Franconian-Bulgar coalition may have prompted Rastislav's desire for an alliance with Byzantium. Realizing that the flux of Frankish missionaries, working among his people, were spreading not only the gospel of Christ, but Frankish influence as well, Rastislav,

Tenth century mosaic set over the south door of the narthex of Hagia Sophia. On the left Justinian I offers his church, and on the right Flavius Valerius Constantinus I, better known as Constantine the Great (311 – 337), offers his city, to the Godbearing Virgin Mary and her Son, enthroned between the two emperors. Photograph by Erich Lessing

aptly referred to as „the Wise" by his Slovak subjects, in about 860 sent a deputation to Rome to Pope Nicholas I, requesting Slavonic speaking teachers and a bishop for his people. The Holy See, while wishing to accede to Rastislav's request, could not, for lack of qualified speakers of the language of the Slovieni. Next Rastislav turned to the Byzantine emperor, Michael III in Constantinople, where his request was rewarded by the dispatch of two brothers, who from that time forth found not only a home in the land of the Slovaks, but a revered and honored place in their history and hearts.

In 863 Constantine-Cyril and Michael-Methodius,[12] usually referred to as Cyril and

---

[12] While no known sources definitively list Methodius' given birth name, claims exist that perhaps it was Michael. See

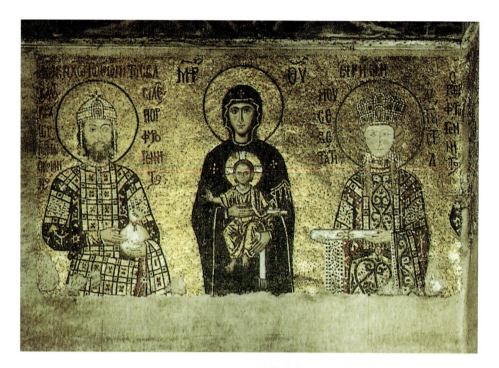

Votive mosaic from the twelfth century, depicting the Theotokos and her Son, between the Emperor John II Comnenus (1118 – 1143) and his wife, Empress Irene (the Princess Piroška, daughter of Ladislav I (1077 – 1095), ruler of the multi-ethnic realm of Hungary), in the south gallery of Hagia Sophia. Photograph by Erich Lessing

The majestically enthroned Godbearer, the Theotokos and her Divine Son, gaze serenely out across the expanse of nave and time, in ethereal and ageless splendor, from the half-dome of the apse of the Great Church of Constantinople. Consecrated by the Patriarch Photius I of Constantinople on March 29, 867 A. D., it is the oldest surviving mosaic in Hagia Sophia. Photograph by Erich Lessing

Methodius or as the *Solúň* Brothers (*Solúň* is the Slovak name for the Greek city of Thessalonika, their birthplace) arrived in the land of the Slovaks and made their way to the court of Prince Rastislav at Nitra. They brought with them not only the Byzantine Codex of civil law, the *Ekloge*, and translations of the gospels and liturgical texts in Old Slavonic, the precursor of modern Slovak, but these words of the Emperor Michael himself to Prince Rastislav, „*Receive this gift, greater and more valuable than all gold and silver, precious stones and transitory riches*"[13] – that gift was the Word of God in their own language. Since no Old Slovak or Slavonic alphabet had existed up to this point, Constantine-Cyril composed[14] by divine revelation tradition says, the Glagolitic (in Slovak, *Hlaholika*) alphabet. Today's Cyrillic alphabet, ascribed to St. Constantine-Cyril, is, in reality, a modification of the Greek alphabet, rather than the Glagolitic alphabet created by St. Cyril, which was adapted for Slavic usage some years after the deaths of Constantine-Cyril and his brother, Methodius.

Rastislav, overjoyed at the arrival of the Thessalonian Brothers in his kingdom, showered them with royal favor and enjoined them to evangelize throughout his realm. The Frankish rulers of the Eastern Mark, however, did not look so favorably upon Prince Rastislav's

Rastislav welcomes St. Constantine-Cyril and St. Methodius. Painting on cloth by Mikuláš Klimčák, 1985. Courtesy of the artist

Peter Arnott, *The Byzantines and Their World* (New York: St. Martin's Press, 1973), p. 155; Michael Lacko, *Saints Cyril and Methodius* (Rome: Slovak Editions, 1969), p. 16; and Laco Zrubec, *Osobnosti našej minulosti* (Bratislava: Slovenské pedagogické nakladateľstvo, 1991), p. 24. Arnott and Zrubec do not state why they think this it is so, but their reasons may be twofold. It was customary for monks of the Greek rite to take a religious name beginning with the same letter as their birth name (Lacko cites this), as Constantine did when he became a monk and took the religious name Cyril which also began with ‚C'. In Methodius' case, all recorded mention of him is long after he become a monk and wherein he is referred to only as Methodius. Had he done the same, his given name would have begun with an ‚M'. Michael was not only a popular name at the time, but also the name of the Byzantine emperor from 811 – 813. Methodius was most likely born between 813 and 815 A. D. Most sources attribute 815 as the year of his birth; however Anton Bagin assigns it to about 813. See Bagin „St. Methodius, Archbishop of Great Moravia." in I. Kružliak and F. Mizenko, eds., *Saints Cyril and Methodius Among the Slovaks* (Middletown: Slovak Catholic Federation, 1985), p. 110. So his birth would have taken place during Michael I's reign, or perhaps shortly thereafter. Thus it is reasonable to assume that that the name of the emperor would be a popular baptismal name for newborn male infants.

[13] Peter P. Yurchak, *The Slovaks* (Whiting: Obrana Press, 1947), p. 50.

[14] Constantine-Cyril, who was a literary figure in his own right, has also left us, among those works of his that have survived, the beautiful, thought provoking piece entitled *The Proglas*, which the present Cardinal-Bishop of Nitra, Ján Chryzostom Korec, himself a prolific author, has referred to as „*a spiritual masterpiece.*"

Svätopluk, King of the Slovaks. Oil painting by Mikuláš Klimčák, 1989. Courtesy of the artist

Mosaic from the latter part of the ninth century, in the north tympanum of Hagia Sophia depicting St. Ignatius the Younger, Patriarch of Constantinople (847 – 858 and 867 – 877). Ignatius, after his father the Emperor Michael I Rhangabe (811 – 813) was deposed, was emasculated to prevent him from pursuing any possible future aspirations to the imperial throne of Byzantium. Instead he rose to the patriarchal throne of Constantinople. About 849 A. D. Constantine the Philosopher was appointed to serve as his chartophylax, a position that combined the functions of both patriarchal secretary and librarian; an office that often led to the patriarchal throne itself. Photograph copyright Calmann & King Ltd, London, reproduced with permission. From Thomas F. Mathews, *Byzantium: From Antiquity to the Renaissance,* 1998

endeavors. His advocation of the Divine Liturgy in the vernacular of his people, instead of the Latin of the Germanic clergy, his preference for Slavonic rather than Frankish culture and the granting of asylum to the German rebel, Albgis, all were distasteful to the Franks. In 864 they made an assault on Rastislav's fortress, the castle of Devín, at the confluence of the Danube

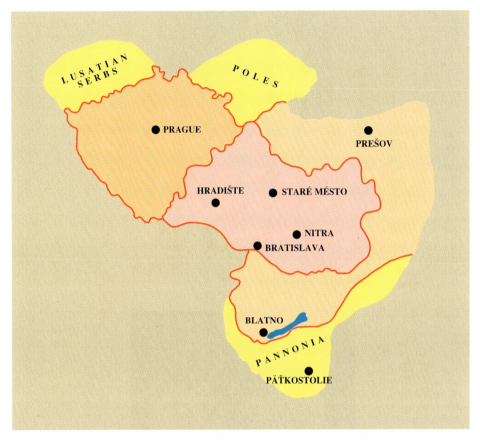

Empire of Veľká Morava – Svätopluk's realm, 870 – 894. Map courtesy of the Matica Slovenská

and Morava Rivers, but a short-term peace was soon achieved along with a transfer of hostages. Rastislav, in the meantime, had enlarged his realm to almost the present-day eastern border of Slovakia and from there as far south as the Danube River. Aroused again, Louis sent his forces, under his son Carloman, against Prince Rastislav in 869. The following year Rastislav fell into Louis' hands through the treachery of his nephew Svätopluk, who had succeeded his uncle as Prince of Nitra. The Franks blinded Rastislav and imprisoned him in the German monastery of Ellwangen, where he died shortly thereafter.

Constantine-Cyril and Methodius likewise did not fare well in the interim. In company

Constantine-Cyril, Methodius and Gorazd. To this triumvirate falls the distinction of having anchored the almost twelve hundred year legacy and history of Christianity in the land of the Slovaks. Painting by Mikuláš Klimčák. Courtesy of the artist

Twentieth century icon, by František Hrtúš, depicting the brothers Constantine-Cyril (827 – 869) and Methodius (813 – 885), the Apostles of the Slovaks and to the Slavs, as well as an alkopion, a ninth century Old Slovak bronze reliquary cross from Veľká Mača, and a Great Moravian basilica. Picture courtesy of Vladimír Čierny, Remium Artistic Productions

with their new proselytes, who were in need of a bishop to ordain them as priests and deacons, the two brothers set off for Venice in 867. They most likely intended to take ship for Constantinople, where their disciples could be ordained, after having been rebuffed by Hermanaric, the Bishop of Passau. Hearing of their sojourn in Venice, Pope Nicholas I invited them to Rome. Upon arriving in the Eternal City, they learned Nicholas had died but were received with high honors by Hadrian II, the new pope, who it is believed, had them housed in the Monastery of St. Praxedes, only a few minutes walking distance from the great Basilica

Twentieth century mosaic of Saint Cyril and Saint Methodius with their disciples, by Jozef Cincík, in the chapel of the Cyrilo-Methodeum Pontifical Slovak College in Rome, Italy. Photograph courtesy of the Pontifical Slovak College of Saint Cyril and St. Methodius, Rome

of Sancta Maria ad Praesepe, situated on the Esquilline Hill, which the Greeks called the Basilica of the Phatne,[15] and is known today as St. Mary Major. Pope Hadrian authorized

---

[15] The Latin word *Praesepe* and the Greek word, *Phatne*, both meaning crib or manger, reflect the fact that, in this basilica, the purported manger in which the newborn Infant Jesus was laid at his birth in Bethlehem was displayed for the viewing of the faithful. Here it remains, still to be seen there today in the confessio located under the high altar. In this basilica, which at various stages has also been known as the *Basilica Liberiana* after Pope Liberius (352 – 366) and *Sancta Maria ad Nives* / Our Lady of the Snows, Hadrian II also authorized the first public celebration of the Slavonic Liturgy. Another interesting fact related to the Basilica of St. Mary Major (its present title of the Great St. Mary's derives from it being the

View of the nave of the Basilica of Saint Praxedes. It is believed that Constantine-Cyril and his brother, Methodius lived in the adjacent monastery during their sojourn in Rome, and where later, before his death, Constantine-Cyril took monastic vows. B. N. Marconi Arte Grafiche, Genoa, Italy

The Basilica of Sancta Praxedes is one of the most ancient of the Roman basilicas, although the first recorded mention of it dates only from 489 A. D. It is dedicated to St. Praxedes (first century), who is thought to have been a daughter of the Roman senator Pudens, mentioned by St. Paul in his second letter to Timothy (4:21). The Basilica's adjoining monastery was a cloister of the monks of the Greek rite in the ninth century and today is under the care of the Vallombrosian Benedictines. Photograph by Andrea Urlandová

not only the ordinations but also the use of their Slavonic Liturgy, which elevated the language of the Slavs to the liturgical heights of Latin, Greek and Hebrew. Sometime thereafter, Constantine fell gravely ill, took monastic vows and the new name of Cyril. Upon his death on February 14, 869, he was interred with great solemnity in the ancient Basilica of St. Clement at the juncture of Via dei Querceti and Via San Giovanni in Laterano, just off the ancient Via Labicana, on the Coelian Hill.

Methodius, whom the pope had created Archbishop-Metropolitan, as well as appointing him a Papal Legate, returned to his labors among the Old Slovaks. There he faced a seemingly endless array of trials and tribulations for the remainder of his life, at the hands of Svätopluk, whom he had rebuked for his sensuous life style, and from the German bishops, who were virulently opposed to the use of the Slavonic Liturgy, not to mention their loss of new lands to proselytize, and the accompanying tithes. Because of its use of the vernacular, the Slavonic Liturgy had met with marked success in converting the people to Christianity. Upon Methodius' death on April 6, 885, he was laid to rest in his episcopal cathedral in the left side of the wall, behind the altar dedicated the Virgin Mary the Godbearer. His funeral service was held in Greek, Latin and Slavonic. To this day neither the location of the church nor the tomb have been identified.[16] Not long afterward, at the

Mounted outside the monastery's main entrance is a sculptured marble plaque, a gift of the Slovak people, in honor of the beloved Thessalonian Brothers. In both the Slovak and the Italian languages, it reads: „In this monastery during the years 867 – 869 resided the Apostles of the Slavs, St. Constantine-Cyril and St. Methodius, the originators of the Old Slavonic Liturgy and Literature. With gratitude from the Slovak Nation." Photograph by Andrea Urlandová

---

largest of all the churches dedicated to the Virgin Mary in Rome), is that the gold used to gild its ceiling was the first gold brought from the Americas and presented as a a gift by King Ferdinand and Queen Isabella of Spain to Pope Alexander VI. It is also one of the four major basilicas of Rome, the others being the basilicas of St. Peter, St. Paul Outside the Walls and St. John Lateran (the Latern Archbasilica, which is actually the Pope's cathedral was originally known as the Basilica of the Holy Saviour and is now dedicated to both St. John the Baptist and St. John the Evangelist. The name Lateran comes from the ancient Roman family of the Laterani, whose palace the original building had been.

[16] Claims have been put forward that Methodius' final resting place was possibly at Mikulčice, Sady or Velehrad, places which have been examined and excavated in detail, but have yielded no concrete proof of such. Furthermore these sites

Entrance to the side Chapel of St. Zeno in the Basilica of Saint Praxedes. The chapel was built by Pope Pascal I (817 – 824) as a mausoleum for his mother Theodora. It is the finest example of ninth century Byzantine art in Rome. B. N. Marconi Arte Grafiche, Genoa, Italy

Mosaic of Christ and angels in the vaulted ceiling of the early ninth century Chapel of Saint Zeno in the Basilica of St. Praxedes in Rome. B. N. Marconi Arte Grafiche, Genoa, Italy

instigation of the German-Ostrogoth bishop Wiching, Methodius' chosen successor Gorazd of Nitra, who in all probability was already Methodius' suffragan, together with his co-religionists Kliment, Angelár, Naum, Vavrinec, Sava and about 200 other Old Slovak clergy of the Slavonic rite, along with several of their followers were shamefully expelled from

Nineteenth century fresco of Constantine-Cyril and Methodius, by Stefano Nobili (1882 – 1886), in the Chapel of Sts. Cyril and Methodius located in the Clementine basilica's upper church. Nobili's work depicts the two Thessalonian brothers' defense of their usage of the Old Slavonic liturgy in the presence of Pope Hadrian II and the Roman Curia. Picture courtesy of the Irish Dominican Fathers, Rome

Svätopluk's lands, and only the Latin rite of the German bishops was given the sanction to continue by Svätopluk.

Svätopluk, the first king of the Slovaks, remains to this day an ambiguous personality. A friend of King Louis' son Carloman, he betrayed his uncle to the Franks and ascended his throne as Svätopluk I. Like his contemporary, the Emperor Basil I, who mounted the throne of the Caesars on the blood of his benefactor, the previous Basileus of the Byzantines,

---

were not ravaged by the Old Hungarians/Magyars during their invasions in the tenth century, as were the Old Slovak sites. The large, thriving major foundations of the Old Slovaks at Bratislava, Devín and Nitra, which were known centers of the ruling classes, on the other hand, also possess the remains of ruined Great Moravian basilics and churches of the Cyrilo-Methodian period. The possibility that Methodius could have been entombed in one of those basilicas or even in one of Pribina's original churches is extremely intriguing.

Ancient mosaic image of Maria Santissima Liberatrice, Our Lady of Deliverance above the altar in the Chapel of St. Zeno in the Basilica of St. Praxedes in Rome. B. N. Marconi Arte Grafiche, Genoa, Italy

The Basilica of Santa Maria Maggiore is among the oldest churches of Rome and one of its four major basilicas. It is the largest of the churches dedicated to the Mother of God, in Rome, whence its name the Great Saint Mary's. Tradition dates it to the reign of Pope Liberius in the fourth century. Photograph courtesy of the College of Santa Maria Maggiore, Rome

Michael III, Svätopluk proved to be a most adept and able ruler. That, however, does not excuse or blot out the stain of regicide. The friendship of Svätopluk and Carloman began deteriorating almost as soon as Svätopluk himself assumed the mantle of kingship. Bringing accusations of disloyalty against him, the Franks seized and imprisoned Svätopluk. The Frankish king, in the meanwhile, appointed two German counts, Wilhelm and Engelschalk, to rule the kingdom of the Slovieni. The Slovaks rose up in rebellion against their new Bavarian masters, and an alarmed Carloman, releasing Svätopluk, sent him at the head of a Frankish army to subdue his countrymen. Turning the tables, Svätopluk, instead of quelling the uprising and delivering the castle-citadel of Devín into the hands of Carloman, joined forces with the rebels and re-took his crown and his kingdom. He now set about extending the borders of his realm. It was, about this time he received the obeisance of the Czech tribes, who recognized him as their sovereign and overlord. In 874, Svätopluk and King Louis signed the Treaty of Forchheim, by which the Franks recognized the independence of Svätopluk's empire. In 880, Svätopluk sent an embassy to Rome, the result of which was Pope John VIII's papal bull „*Industriae Tuae*", which established Nitra as the first Slovak, as well as the premier Slavic, bishopric, recognized Old Slavonic, the forerunner of modern Slovak and its sister tongues, as a liturgical language alongside Latin, Greek and Hebrew and acknowledged the kingship of Svätopluk. Svätopluk had succeeded in uniting under his banner, not only the Slovaks and the Moravians, but the Lusatian Serbs and the Silesians as well as the Czech tribes. In 894, Svätopluk the Great died, and his empire passed into the hands of his three sons, Mojmír II, Svätopluk II and Prince Bratslav,[17] whose memory lives on in the

View of the high altar of St. Mary Major with its great porphyry columned ciborium. It was at the high altar of the Great St. Mary's Basilica that Pope Hadrian II authorized the first public liturgy in Old Slavonic to be celebrated by Constantine the Philosopher, Methodius and the Roman clergy in 868. Photograph courtesy of the College of Santa Maria Maggiore, Rome

---

[17] Several sources give variations, or even a totally different name for Bratslav, the son of Svätopluk I. Some of those other names are Predslav/Preslav and Svätoboj; see Peter Yurchak, *The Slovaks* (Whiting: Obrana Press, 1946) p. 390; and

The marble commemorative plague, sculpted by Marián Polonský, in the baptistry of the Basilica of Santa Maria Maggiore in Rome was dedicated in 1998 in honor of Constantine-Cyril and Methodius. A gift of the people of Slovakia, the English translation of its Slovak and Italian text reads – „In this Basilica, in the year 868, Pope Hadrian II blessed and approved the Old Slavonic Liturgical Books of the Apostles of the Slavs, St. Constantine-Cyril and St. Methodius. In gratitude from the Slovak Nation."
Photograph by Andrea Urlandová

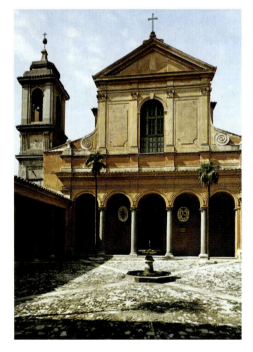

View of the atrium and façade of the Basilica of San Clemente in Rome. The Basilica is dedicated to the fourth pope, Clement (88 – 97 A.D.), who, it is thought, was associated with the noble gens Flavii, and who died in exile in the Crimea. It is under the care of the Irish Dominicans. The presumed relics of St. Clement were discovered, miraculously as it is said, by Constantine-Cyril on an island off the coast of Cherson during the winter of 860 – 861. They were brought by him and his brother Methodius to Rome in 867 A.D. and placed in the Clementine Basilica.
Photograph courtesy of the Irish Dominican Fathers, Rome

name of Slovakia's capital city of Bratislava.¹⁸ A legend claims that on his deathbed Svätopluk gathered his sons around him and gave each of them a stick to break, which they easily did. He then gave each of them a bundle of sticks, bound together, which could not so easily be broken. The lesson to be learned being that if his sons, among who he had divided his kingdom, remained unified, they would hopefully withstand the attempts of their enemies to overrun their kingdoms. Although Mojmír and Bratslav maintained good relations with one another, this was not the case with Svätopluk II and his brothers. Factional rivalries and differences soon began to fracture the structure of their father's empire.

In 895, the Czechs, under their tribal chieftain Spytihnev, defected from the suzerainty of the Svätopluk dynasty and submitted themselves in feudal vassalage to the Frankish-German king at Regensburg. The defection of the Czech tribes as well as the integration of Cracovia into the emerging Polish state left the kingdom of the Slovieni much weakened, and now sandwiched between the threatening armies of the Frankish-Germans and Magyar-Hungarians.

Magyar hordes, from the east, had

View looking down the nave towards the high altar of the twelfth century Basilica of St. Clement, with its celebrated ambos, paschal candlestick and schola cantorum from the fourth century lower church. At the beginning of the eighteenth century, during the pontificate of Pope Clement XI (1702 – 1715), the interior was renovated to its present state. Photograph courtesy of the Irish Dominican Fathers, Rome

---

Rudolf Krajčovič, *Veľká Morava v tisícročí* (Bratislava: Tatran, 1985) p. 120. Svätopluk I is also credited with a daughter called Devojna supposedly named in honor of Devín; see Stephen J. Palickar, *Slovakian Culture in the Light of History* (Cambridge: The Hampshire Press, 1954) p. 43.

¹⁸ Joseph Cincik, *One Hunderd Famous Slovak Men* (Cambridge: Friends of Good Books, 1984) pp. 22, 29 – 33. Palickar, p. 48. See Špetko, „The Christianization of the Slovieni in the Pre-Cyrillo-Methodian Era" in Kružliak and Mizenko, eds., p. 43, refers to the earliest name for Bratislava as the Castle of Vratislav. Two Frankish names for Bratislava Castle are Brezalauspurch and Pressalauspurch, which in translation are construed as Bratslav's Castle or Preslav's Castle, for the former see Peter Baxa and Viktor Ferus, *Bratislava mešťana Wocha* (Prievidza: Tlačiareň Patria, 1991) p. 4, and for the latter see Štefan Holčík and Tatiana Štefanovičová, *The Castle of Bratislava* (Bratislava: Obzor, 1982) p. 19. The Austrians have consistently used the term Pressburg, i. e. *Brezalauspurch/Pressalauspurch* for the Slovak Capital. The Magyar-Hungarian term Pozsony is a corruption of *Posonium,* an Old Roman name for Bratislava. Roman outposts and/or towns along or near the Danubian highway included *Vindobona*/Vienna; *Carnuntum*/Petronell; Posonium or Istropolis/Bratislava; *Gerulata*/Rusovce; *Brigetium*/Komárno; *Acquincum*/Budapest and *Singidunum*/Belgrade among others.

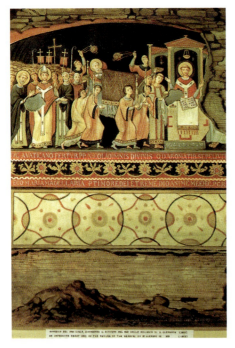

A nineteenth century reproduction of an eleventh century fresco in the narthex of the fourth century church of St. Clement. The fresco depicts a portion of the ceremonies in connection with the transfer of the remains of Pope St. Clement, from St. Peter's Basilica to the Clementine basilica in 868 A. D. Photograph courtesy of the Irish Dominican Fathers, Rome

Detail from the original eleventh century fresco depicting Constantine-Cyril and Methodius in procession with Pope Hadrian II, during the transfer of the relics of St. Clement. Photograph courtesy of the Irish Dominican Fathers, Rome

A sixth century Byzantine style fresco of the Mother of God and her Divine Son, in the north aisle of the lower church of St. Clement in Rome. It has been suggested that it is possibly a contemporary portrait of the Empress Theodora (527 – 548 A. D.), wife of Justinian I (527 – 565 A. D.), which was altered to its present state in the ninth century. Photograph courtesy of the Irish Dominican Fathers, Rome

crossed the Tisa River into Slovakia in 896, and had been steadily encroaching on Slovak territory ever since. Tradition holds that on or about July 4, 907, the Battle of Bratislava was fought, under the ramparts of Bratslav's castle, dealing the death blow to the empire of the Slovieni. The Magyars were victorious and the kingdom of Slovakia would eventually be incorporated as a province into what, in time, would become the kingdom of *Uhorsko*,[19] often referred to by its Latin name of Hungaria. For the *People of the Word* and Slovakia, a long dark night had begun.

---

[19] Uhorsko, the name for the former kingdom of Hungary takes its name from the Uhri/Ugri, an Asiatic group akin to the Samoyeds of Northeastern Siberia; the ancestors of the Magyars. Uhorsko, as well as the current terms Maďarsko and Magyarország that are used for presentday Hungary, are all rendered in English translation as Hungary. In the interest of clarity it should be pointed out that the use of the word Hungarian, to describe a citizen of the Hungarian kingdom, does not necessarily mean that the person is an ethnic Hungarian-Magyar but rather a citizen of the Hungarian kingdom, who in many cases belonged to one of the other ethnic groups that comprised the multi-ethnic kingdom of Hungary. The description Hungarian may well be correlated to the use of the word American which describes all the citizens of the United States but does not take into account their ethnic origins.

Our Lord's Descent into Limbo, a ninth century fresco in the south aisle of the lower fourth century Clementine Basilica. Photograph courtesy of the Irish Dominican Fathers, Rome

Depiction of St. Constantine-Cyril on the lower left hand side of the Lord's Descent into Limbo fresco in St. Clement's Basilica. Photograph courtesy of the Irish Dominican Fathers, Rome

Tomb and detail of a mosaic of St. Constantine-Cyril located in the south aisle of the Clementine Basilica's fourth century lower church. The upper church dates from the twelfth century. Constantine-Cyril died in Rome on February 14, 869 and was interred in the Clementine Basilica. His tomb attracts pilgrims from around the world. The altar over it was a gift of the Slovaks of the United States of America in 1952. Photograph courtesy of the Irish Dominican Fathers, Rome

Sculpture of Saint Cyril and Saint Methodius by Viliam Schiffer, in the courtyard of the Cyrilo-Methodeum Slovak Pontifical College in Rome. Photograph by Paul Gallo

Byzantine pyxidium, of ivory, approximately four inches in height and five inches in diameter, circa 330 A. D., part of the Great Moravian Collection of the Municipal Museum of Nitra. Probably created to commemorate the foundation of Constantinople on May 11, 330 A. D. and discovered at Čierne Kľačany near Nitra in Slovakia. It is believed to have been brought as a gift, from the Emperor Michael III to Prince Rastislav, by Constantine-Cyril and Methodius when they and the Byzantine Mission arrived in Nitra in 863 A. D. Photograph courtesy of the Nitra Information System Office

A page from the thirteenth century Hlaholské listy Hlohovské, the Hlohovec Glagolitic Document. Originally part of the library of the Franciscan Monastery of All Saints in Hlohovec, it is now the oldest extent hand-written Glagolitic manuscript in the Matica Slovenská's collection of incunabula. Photograph by Alexander Psica

Restored ninth century Great Moravian church and chapel foundations on the castle mount of Devín. Photograph courtesy of the Matica slovenská, from: Kultúrne dedičstvo Slovenska

Scuplture of the Solúň brothers, Constantine-Cyril (827 – 869) and Methodius (815 – 885), by Ľudmila Cvengrošová near the main entrance to the Castle of Nitra. Photograph courtesy of the Nitra Information System Office

King Svätopluk, on his deathbed, instructs his sons, Mojmír II, Svätopluk II and Bratslav, by means of the Tale of the Three Twigs, that strength lies in unity. Painting by Maximilián Schurmann. Courtesy of JUDr. Štefan Valent. Photograph by Marta Novotná

The baroque interior and main altar of Nitra's Cathedral of St. Emeram located on the castle mount. During the thirteenth century, the ninth century Romanesque church was rebuilt in the gothic style. Later eighteenth century renovations again changed the cathedral's appearance to its present baroque style. Photograph by Marta Novotná

The Municipal Coat-of Arms of Nitra. Courtesy of the City of Nitra

CHAPTER THREE

The Tenth through the Fifteenth Centuries

With the destruction of the Great Moravian Empire by the Magyar hordes in 907 A.D., the flower of the Slovakian nobility and intelligentsia was decimated. Prince Bratslav himself disappears from the chroniclers' accounts of history at this point; and it is said that he bravely went down under the swords of his enemies, beneath the ramparts of his castle, defending his Slovak homeland. The remaining Slovak aristocratic families, who had escaped the slaughter below Bratislava Castle, found sanctuary in the fastness of their mountain fortresses or escaped into exile. A pall had settled over the land; the auspicious, burgeoning golden age of Slovakia's Great Moravian Empire was cut down in the bloom of its youthful beginnings.

Slovakia, in the tenth century, became a bloody stage on which the power plays of the Slovaks, the Franks and the Magyars were enacted. At last, in 955, on the Lechfeld near Augsburg, the German king Otto I so decisively defeated the Magyars that they never were a threat again. Unfortunately for the Slovaks, their defeat came forty-eight years too late. Vanquished, the Magyars turned from wandering marauders to a more stationary life-style. In spite of the unsettled times, widespread devastation and systematic raiding and wars, the Christian Slovaks, though overrun by the pagan Magyars had, by the eleventh century, succeeded in civilizing and Christianizing their formerly discursive, new masters. In the process, the Magyar language borrowed many basic terms and words from Slovak, albeit Magyarizing them to various degrees. A few examples[20] are listed herewith:

Slovak	Magyar	English
kráľ	király	king
župan	ispán	administrative chief
slama	szalma	straw
seno	széna	hay
brázda	barázda	furrow
stolár	astalos	cabinet maker
mäsiar	mészáros	butcher
podkova	patkó	horseshoe
kováč	kovacs	blacksmith
štvrtok	csztÎrÎk	Thursday
piatok	péntek	Friday
milosť	malaszt	grace
oblok	ablak	window
pohár	pohár	goblet
brána	borona	gate

These, and a host of other Slovak words, found their way into the vocabulary of the Magyars during their transition from a nomadic to a more sedentary life. (The linguist will easily be able to corroborate the Slavonic-Slovak origin of these words, as their counterparts in the other Slavic/Indo-European languages are extremely similar, this not being the case in the non-Indo-European Magyar language.)

In the eleventh century, under the Arpád clan, a new multi-ethnic political entity, the kingdom of Hungary had risen on the ruins of the former Great Moravian territories of Slovakia and Pannonia. It was part of the Arpád dynasty's program to encourage the immigration to, and the colonization of, the lands under their sway, by German immigrants. The motivation for this policy appears to have been twofold. On the one hand, the incoming immigrants would bring needed skills and industry to their new homeland and, on the other, they would increase the number of defenders of the embryonic multinational Hungarian state against other nomadic invaders from the East. The new Magyar masters had not forgotten how they had gained their present territories. The cities under the Hungarian crown were granted royal charters from the kings and acted as a counter balance for the

---

[20] Thomas Capek, *The Slovaks of Hungary* (New York: The Knickerbocker Press, 1906) p. 174.

monarch against the noble classes. The towns however, were not allowed to participate overmuch on the political scene; that remained the domain of kings, princes and palatines.

Adding to the problems of the new multi-ethnic Hungarian state of the eleventh century were a number of pagan Magyar insurrections that took place after the death of Stephen I. Within the same time frame attempts were also made by the German emperors Henry III and Henry IV to attach the area to their domains. To neutralize those attempts, Gejza I presented the kingdom to Pope Gregory VII and then received it back from him, to be held as a papal fief.

During this period, when almost all of Europe was occupied as well with the Crusades

Multi-ethnic Kingdom of Hungary 10th – 12th century. Map courtesy of the Matica Slovenská

that took place from 1096 – 1270, it is believed the Knights Templar also established themselves, on the territory of Slovakia, most notably in the areas of Turiec and Liptov. The first Crusade occurred during the reign of the Byzantine Emperor Alexius I Comnenus and the papacy of Urban II; the last one, advocated by King Louis IX of France, when Michael VIII Palaeologus ruled in Constantinople and the papal throne sat unoccupied for almost a three year period. The daring and deeds of the Templars, whom the Slovaks called the *Červení mnísi*/the Red Monks because of the red crosses emblazoned on their cloaks and tunics, inspired a number of Slovak tales and legends about the exploits of these brave and fearless knights, who later came to be unjustly maligned and persecuted by the French king Philip IV.

The Castle of Spiš, twelfth century. Picture courtesy of the Matica Slovenská

Two of the many medieval defense citadels and castles that dot the Slovakian landscape.

The Castle of Bytča, thirteenth century. Picture courtesy of the Matica Slovenská

The Magyars had just about settled into ruling the lands of Slovakia and Pannonia that they had wrested from Great Moravia when in 1241 the Tatars invaded and overran the Hungarian lands. The carnage of the Battle of Mohi, where the forces of Batu Khan obliterated, almost in its entirety, the Hungarian military was a catastrophe of major proportion for the kingdom. The Mongolian Tatars, bloodbrothers of the Mongolian Magyars, ravaged anew the land the Magyars had seized from the Slovaks. At the Battle of the Slaná River, King Belo IV was defeated and driven into exile. Batu took both Pest and Ostrihom, and occupied most of

The Castle of Trenčín was built in the eleventh century near the site of the second century A. D. Roman castellum of Laugaricio. In the latter part of the thirteenth century, it was the seat of the palatine, Matúš Čak Trenčiansky, the Lord of the Váh and the Tatras. Picture courtesy of the Matica Slovenská

Pannonia. The Tatars also raided and plundered the environs of Bratislava and other parts of Slovakia proper as well. Upon the death of their great khan Ogadai, the son of Genghis, Batu and his Tatars hastily returned to the East to elect a new leader. King Belo, returning from exile, paid special attention to re-fortifying his realms, constructing new and restoring many of the old, fortresses and keeps. It was at this time that many of the great ruined castles, that now so picturesquely dot the Slovakian landscape, were built.

In 1301, Andrew III, the last king of the Arpád dynasty, died without male issue and thus opened the way to the throne for three claimants from the female branch of the line –

Otto of Bavaria, Václav of Bohemia and Charles Robert of Anjou. One of the greatest Slovak palatines, land magnates, at this time, was Matúš Čak Trenčiansky. Technically, the „uncrowned" king of Slovakia, he had, by skillfully playing off one contender against the other, been able to maintain, and then extend the borders of his territory. He effectively ruled over twelve of the nineteen Slovak counties from his castle at Trenčín, and held thirty Slovak castles and fortresses under his jurisdiction. An astute politician who used all the wiles he could command, pitting faction against faction, to maintain his power, he eventually

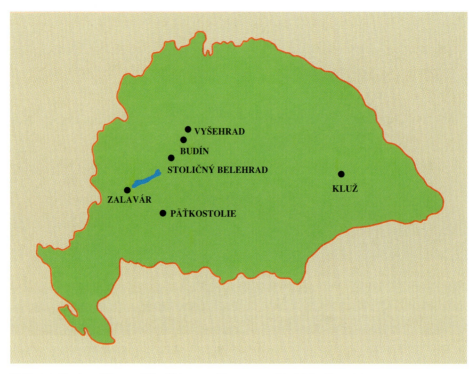

Multi-ethnic Kingdom of Hungary 14th – 15th century. Map courtesy of the Matica Slovenská

fell out of favor with King Charles Robert, who sought to destroy Čak, whose sobriquet had become „the Lord of the Váh and the Tatras." On June 15, 1312, the armies of Matúš Čak and Charles Robert finally clashed, in the vicinity of Košice, at Rozhanovce by the Torysa River. Matúš Čak's army, although greatly outnumbered, fought well and courageously, but were overwhelmed and defeated by the troops of the king. History does not specifically record that Matúš Čak desired the crown of Slovakia, but on that fatal day, on the battlefield of Rozhanovce, perished not only the dreams of Matúš Čak, but any chance of a sovereign Slovakia until the twentieth century.

The 1300s gave way to the 1400s and with it the advent of the Hussite wars. Upon the death of Albert of Habsburg in 1439, a new war of succession flared up. Many Slovaks ranged themselves on the side of his widow Elizabeth and her son Ladislav the Posthumous. Most of the Hungarians favored the rival candidate Vladislav, the King of Poland. Civil war waged mercilessly, and even though the Slovaks had sided with the cause of Queen Elizabeth, her army of Hussite mercenaries, who had been under the command of Jan Jiskra of Brandýs, looted, pillaged and destroyed many Slovak churches, towns and monasteries. In 1444, King Vladislav fell at the Battle of Varna, engaged in the war against the Turks. With his demise, the Hungarian Estates recognized Ladislav the Posthumous as king, with Ján Hunyady as regent. Peace, however, did not fully ensue until Ladislav himself was old enough to assume the throne, because of the mutual animosity Hunyady and Jiskra shared for one another.

On a more positive note, in the year 1465 the first university in Bratislava, the Academia Istropolitana, was founded by King Matthias Corvinus. Students accepted there were able to study in the fields of law, medicine, theology and the arts.

The discord of the 1400s flowed almost unhindered into the 1500s. The most memorable date which affected Slovak history is the 29th of August, 1526. It marks the Battle of Mohács and the Turkish invasion of Central Europe and Slovakia. On May 28, 1453, to the consternation of Europe, the grand city of Constantinople, for over a thousand years the bulwark of Christianity on the shores of the Bosphorus, fell to the infidel Turks and their sultan Mohammed II. In what can only be called a sardonic twist of fate, it was the Hungarian envoy[21] to the sultan who, effectively, showed the Turkish artillery how to breach the great land walls that led to the fall of the „Queen of Cities", and

The Castle of Topoľčany, thirteenth century. Photograph courtesy of the Matica Slovenská

---

[21] George Young, *Constantinople* (New York: Barnes and Noble, 1992) p. 120. Paul Hetherington and Werner Forman, *Byzantium: City of Gold, City of Faith* (London: Orbis, 1988) p. 112. Edwin A. Grosvenor, *Constantinople* (Boston: Roberts Brothers, 1895) II, p. 610. Grosvenor refers to the Hungarian cannon engineer Urban as Ourban (sic) and states he was a mercenary who, for more money, had deserted the Byzantine emperor to serve the Turkish sultan.

The Castle of Strečno, thirteenth century. Photograph courtesy of the Matica Slovenská

Košice's thirteenth century Cathedral of St. Elizabeth, built circa 1283. The City of Košice is today the second largest city in Slovakia. Photograph courtesy of the Matica Slovenská, from: Kultúrne dedičstvo Slovenska

The Municipal Coat-of-Arms of Košice. Courtesy of the Matica Slovenská

the reduction of its population by 90 per cent, from 100,000 Christians to 10,000, through either death or enslavement. In less than seventy-five years the Turks would invade Central Europe, unsheathing their attempts at western conquest. And where the last blood of the Eastern Roman Empire had flowed so freely, at the Gates of Byzantium, trying to stem the Turkish tide rushing down on them, it would now, ironically, be a great deal of Hungarian blood that would flow, in the field of Mohács, as they tried to close the floodgates they had helped to open. The massacre at Mohács, of the forces of the Hungarian state, left the way to Europe wide open for the victorious Turkish armies of Suleiman I, and it was not until the Turks, along with their Hungarian allies, were defeated at the gates of Vienna on September 12, 1683, that Christian Europe again breathed easy, delivered from the Turkish threat. Budapest fell to Suleiman on September 10, 1526, not quite two weeks after the battle of Mohács, and those Hungarians who chose not to live under the Turkish yoke, and who were able to flee, quickly retreated to Bratislava, which would become the Hungarians' capital in exile. Slovakia, likewise, bore the brunt of Turkish raids, looting and plundering on its territory proper until the armies under the command of King John Sobieski of Poland and Duke Charles V of Lorraine saved Europe for Christianity, under the walls of Vienna, on that mid-September day in 1683. The terror and savagery of the Turkish invasion and wars left such an impact on the Slovak populace that even into the 1800s, the collective Slovak memory retained the horror of those times in many Slovak folk and religious songs produced by a scarred Slovak national psyche.

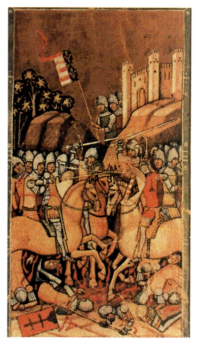

Medieval depiction of the Battle of Rozhanovce on June 15, 1312 where the armies of of Matúš Čak Trenčiansky and Charles Robert of Anjou clashed on the banks of the River Torysa. From The Vienna Pictorial Chronicles. Picture courtesy of the Matica Slovenská

The 1500s also produced the Augustinian monk Martin Luther, who with the posting of his ninety-five theses attacking the use of indulgences and their doctrinal basis on the doors of the Castle Church at Wittenberg, Germany, on October 31, 1517, ignited the Protestant Reformation and the Catholic Counter-Reformation, both of which, to varying degrees, would affect Slovak history.

Matúš Čak Trenčiansky (1260 – 1321), Lord of the Váh and the Tatras. Painting by Ivan Pavlisko

Matthias Corvinus (1440 – 1490), King of Hungary. Picture courtesy of the Matica Slovenská

CHAPTER FOUR

The Sixteenth through the Eighteenth Centuries

The sixteenth century found Slovakia and Europe racked not only by the religious dissension that would culminate in the Protestant Reformation and the Catholic Counter-Reformation, but under siege by the aggressive Islamic forces of the Turkish sultanate. Of the divisive religious and moral issues that splintered European Christendom at this time, tomes have been written, wars waged and the human condition debased and enhanced by the causes and effects of both undertakings. The mating of religious assent, or dissent, and politics among the ruling princes of the European kingdoms was embodied in the establishment of denominational Christian zones by the de facto policy subscribed to, in the phrase „*cuius regio eius religio/The ruler's religion is the realm's religion.*" Toleration was far from the norm, and in effect it was the ruling princes who gained the most, as they, for the most part, now chose what the state church would be and who would be appointed to its clergy and ministers. The Thirty Years War, which occupied approximately a third of the seventeenth century (1618 – 1648) with its brutality and intolerance, began as a war of religious enmity, and wreaked havoc throughout Slovakia and Central Europe. During its course, the war's focus had shifted to the diverse ambitions of a variety of royal dynasties, envious of the power and might of the Habsburg emperors, who now sought to check that power and might. It must be factually stated that the general Slovak populace suffered tremendously and indiscriminately at the hands of all the various factions engaged in prosecuting the Thirty Years War on Slovak soil. The Peace of Westphalia, which concluded the war, was signed on October 24, 1648. It providently allowed Europe the necessary time to prepare itself for the coming onslaught of the armies of the Turkish sultan Mohammed IV.

With the Fall of Constantinople in 1453, the Ottoman Turks set their sights on expansion in Europe at the expense of the kingdoms of central, southern and eastern Europe. The years 1526 to 1683 mark the „Period of the Turkish Terror", which commenced with

Austria and Hungary 1526 – 1795. Map courtesy of the Matica Slovenská

the Battle of Mohács and began its decline with the destruction of the Turkish army, together with their Hungarian allies, at the gates of Vienna. The soil of Slovakia soaked up the blood of her children as the Turks laid waste the land. Among the Slovak cities taken, pillaged and torched by the Turkish invaders in their assault of 1663 were Štúrovo in March, Hlohovec on September 3rd, Nové Zámky on September 15th, Nitra in October, Levice on November 3rd, Novohrad on November 17th as well as the towns of Bujak, Fiľakovo and Sučany. The fall of the fortress-citadel of Hlohovec was a particularly great loss, as it guarded the lower Váh River valley above the confluence of the Váh and Danube Rivers. Slovakia once again became a battleground where, for twenty years, outside forces strove to sate their lust for power.

Toward the end of the summer of 1683, a Muslim Turkish army consisting of about 250,000 soldiers, under the command of the Ottoman Grand Vizier Kara Mustafa marched against the city of Vienna. Rushing to join him, the Turks' Hungarian allies under the command of Imre Thököly were defeated near Bratislava. And on September 12, 1683, the army of the Holy Roman Empire together with the army of the Kingdom of Poland and other volunteer European units, vanquished Mohammed IV's army of depredation and saved Europe from the Turkish onslaught. Christianity, although fragmented after the Reformation and the Counter-Reformation, and shackled here and there by the Turkish wars of conquest, had survived and entered eighteenth century European life as a still viable force. In all fairness it must be said that Slovakia and the Slovaks were not exploited and ravaged solely by the Turks, but by the Christian armies as well during the time of the Turkish troubles. Even Slovakia's northernmost region felt the sting of the oppressor's sword as the Lithuanian forces of Casimir Sapieha looted and plundered their way through Orava, after the Battle of Vienna, pillaging and burning the village of Habovka together with twenty-four other Oravan villages, before turning their rapacious attention to the Váh valley, during the spoliations of 1683.

The Castle of Hlohovec, overlooking the River Váh, was first mentioned in 870 – 880, by the Frankish chroniclers in the Annals of Fulda. Photograph by Alexander Psica

In the seventeenth century Slovakia had to endure not only the Turkish invasions, but a protracted series of anti-Habsburg rebellions, frequently referred to as the Class Wars. These revolts which ranged a number of the higher nobility against the emperor took place almost continuously throughout the century, with the last one coming to an end in the year 1711. As elsewhere, they were often drawn along the lines of religious convictions.

The likes of such great landowning magnates and palatines as Štefan Bocskay, Juraj Rákoci I and Juraj Rákoci II, Imre Thököly, František Rákoci and Gábor Bethlen pitted themselves against the Imperial Crown. These upheavals, some of which were fought during

Built in 1242, Hlohovec's thirteenth century Gothic Church of St. Michael the Archangel dominates the city's main square. Photograph by Alexander Psica

View looking down the nave toward the main altar of the Church of St. Michael the Archangel in Hlohovec. Photograph by Alexander Psica

and within the context of the Thirty Years War, for the most part were focused on the magnates' desire to retain or gain certain rights and prerogatives. In the end the Crown prevailed, and by means of diplomacy, might and arbitration it maintained, and strengthened Habsburg royal supremacy and authority.

The late seventeenth century also produced that „*king of Slovak folk heroes*", Slovakia's pride and joy, the legendary Juraj Jánošík, who according to the many tales and fables surrounding this most beloved hero of the Slovak nation, „robbed from the rich and gave to the poor". He was born on January 25, 1688 in the village of Terchová in Trenčín County, where his family was bound in serfdom to the feudal lords of Veľká Bytča. Supposedly after taking revenge on his masters for various outrages committed against his family, including the torturing of his father on the rack, he took refuge in the dense forests and wild mountains of Slovakia. He attracted a following of outlaws like himself to his mountain strongholds and began a career that enshrined him in the hearts of the Slovak people and their folklore as a stalwart symbol of defiance to oppressive tyranny and a champion against injustice. Then his short, but active life ended with his capture and execution on March 18, 1713, in Liptovský Svätý Mikuláš, by hanging. The Slovak poet Ján Botto (1829 – 1881) helped immortalize the great Slovak folk hero through his magnificent epic poem „*Smrť Jánošíkova / The Death of Jánošík*".

Fresco of St. Cyril & St. Methodius in the Church of St. Michael the Archangel in Hlohovec. Photograph by Alexander Psica

The eighteenth century in Slovakia saw the use of the first steam engine, in 1722, in the city of Banská Štiavnica and likewise the founding of the world's premier Mining Academy in that same city in 1762. It also witnessed the birth in Slanica, Orava County, of Anton Bernolák (1762 – 1813). Bernolák, who later became a Catholic priest, was the first person to codify the Slovak language. The western Slovak dialect he used as the basis for literary Slovak was used until 1851, when both Catholic and Protestant Slovaks agreed that the two groups would use the central Slovakian dialect which Ľudovít Štúr had proposed and promoted.

The Franciscan Monastery of All Saints in the city of Hlohovec was founded by the Friars Minor between 1465 – 1492 A. D. Photograph by Alexander Psica

Interior view of the fifteenth century All Saints Franciscan Monastery Church looking towards the main altar. Photograph by Alexander Psica

The Municipal Coat-of-Arms of Hlohovec. Courtesy of the City of Hlohovec

A growing interest in Slovakia's ancient heritage started to take hold among the people. Works like „*About the Kingdom and the Kings of the Slovaks*" by Juraj Papánek (1780) and Juraj Sklenár's „*About the Oldest Site of Great Moravia*" (1784) helped spark renewed interest in Slovak origins. Together with Anton Bernolák's labors and codification of the Slovak language in his „*Grammatica Slavica*" (1790), they helped to set the stage for the establishment of the *Slovenské učené tovaryšstvo/The Slovak Learned Society* (1792) and the birth of the Slovak National Revival in the nineteenth century. The brightness of a new dawn had finally begun to dispel the dark, black night that had settled for so long over Slovakia and the Slovak nation.

Situated on the region's historic Amber Route, the Castle of Orava rises high on a promontory overlooking the Orava River. First mention of it is in documents dating from 1267. Painting by Panuška

Orava Castle. View of the main courtyard. Oil painting by an unknown artist. Picture courtesy of the Orava Art Gallery, Dolný Kubín

The Village of Habovka in Orava, established in 1593 and nestled in the Studená valley forms part of the gateway to the magnificent Western High Tatra Mountain areas of the Oravice and Roháče. Photograph by Lýdia Vojtaššáková

Detailed view of the upper and middle castle from its main courtyard. The division of Orava Castle into three sections, referred to as the upper, middle and lower castle, is along its lines of elevation rather than of any particular architectural expansion. Photograph by Lýdia Vojtaššáková

The village Church of Panna Mária Sedembolestná, Our Lady of the Seven Sorrows, Patroness of Slovakia, in Habovka, Orava, was constructed between 1817 – 1829. Photograph by Lýdia Vojtaššáková

Perched on a bluff overlooking the village, Habovka's nineteenth century Chapel of St. Mária Magdaléna was built in 1856. Photograph by Lýdia Vojtaššáková

The pristine beauty of Orava's western High Tatra mountain range, Europe's second highest, delights its visitors year 'round, whether basking in the rays of the summer sun or in a cover of winter snow. Summer scene. Photograph by Lýdia Vojtaššáková. Winter scene. Photograph by Vladimír Žuffa

Harvestime haystacks outside of the village of Habovka blend with field, mountain and sky to celebrate the beauty of the Slovak countryside. Photograph by Lýdia Vojtaššáková

The Municipal Coat-of-Arms of Habovka.
Courtesy of the Matica Slovenská

Three views of Roháče and the majestic western High Tatras mounatins of Slovakia.
Photographs by Vladimír Žuffa

Juraj Jánošík receiving the magic shirt, the magic belt and the magic valaška (highlander's ax) as gifts from the three forest nymphs. Painting by Martin Benka. Picture courtesy of the Slovenské národné múzeum – Múzeum Martina Benku, Martin

Jánošík's farewell address from the gallows. Painting in tempera by Mikuláš Klimčák. Courtesy of the Artist

Juraj Janošík (1688 – 1713). Painting by Ivan Pavlisko

Anton Bernolák (1762 – 1813), First Codifier of the Slovak Language. Painting by Ivan Pavlisko

CHAPTER FIVE

The Nineteenth Century

Although serfdom had been abrogated in the Habsburg lands in the year 1785, it was not until 1848 that it was abolished in the lands under the sway of Hungary. And perhaps to counter the loss of their Slovak, and other serfs, such as the Rusins, Croatians, Romanians, etc., the Hungarian government now instituted an ironfisted policy of Magyarization. The official language of the multinational, polyglot kingdom of Hungary had always been Latin, which also as a church language and the *lingua franca* of the realm had bound together the numerous peoples of which the kingdom of Hungary was comprised. The Hungarian government began a policy of Magyarization of the non-Magyar nationalities, under their jurisdiction, with a ruthless proscription of their languages and cultures. Those repressive policies would widen an already deepening chasm between the Slovaks and the Magyar-Hungarians, the backlash of which would give rise to a fearless new class of Slovak intellectuals and a new sense of historic consciousness to the Slovak nation.

Nevertheless, the nineteenth century in Slovakia witnessed such an outpouring of Slovak intellectual activity and literary creativity that it is heralded as the period of the re-birth of Slovak national consciousness. It likewise brought to maturity the time frame assigned the name, the Slovak National Revival, which began in the eighteenth century and extended into the early twentieth century. The new breed of Slovak intelligentsia, was composed of, but not limited to, such notables as Anton

Bernolák, Samoslav Chalupka, Ján Hollý, Jozef Miloslav Hurban, Pavol Országh Hviezdoslav, Ján Kollár, Janko Kráľ, Martin Kukučín, Štefan Moyses, Pavol Jozef Šafárik, Andrej Sládkovič, Ľudovít Štúr and Svetozár Hurban Vajanský. Their endeavors and writings, to name but a few, include, Chalupka's *Mor ho, Smútok* and *Bolo i bude*, Hollý's epic works *Svätopluk, Cyrilo-Methodiada* and *Slav*, Slovakia's poet laureate, Hviezdoslav's *Rastislav, Krvavé sonety/Bloody Sonnets* and the lyrical epic *Hájnikova žena/ The Forester's Wife*, Kollár's *Slávy dcera/Daughter of Glory*, Sládkovič's magnificient narrative poems *Detvan* and *Marína* and Štúr's *The Theory of the Slovak Language*. Unfortunately much of Slovakia's treasure trove of great literary pieces have not as yet been translated from Slovak into English.

Among all the illustrious personalities mentioned above, a special note should be made of Ľudovít Štúr (1815 – 1856), who was born in the village of Uhrovec.[22] Within Štúr's short life span his efforts led to the establishment of a central Slovakian dialect as the grammatical Slovak language that forms the basis of modern Slovak. Because of his literary achievements and leadership qualities, in the revolutionary uprising of 1848 – 1849, he ranks among Slovakia's most revered patriots.

It is indeed a truly amazing accomplishment and tribute to the ingenuity and abilities of the Slovak intelligentsia of the times, that such a flowering of Slovak literature occurred during a period that also spawned the ruthless and ironfisted Magyarization policies of Slovakia's foreign rulers in Budapest. And this, at a time when even the term „*the Slovak nation*" was proscribed by the Hungarian government, and in point of law, even forbidden to be used within the confines of the Hungarian kingdom. A kingdom that also included the venerable homeland of the Slovak people, *Slovensko*, which the Hungarian government arrogantly preferred to refer to as Upper Hungary, instead of by its ancient name of Slovakia.

It was not, however, just from the ranks of literary personages that Slovakia drew the defenders of her people's rights and cause against the tyranny of the Hungarian government. Men such as Štefan Marko Daxner, who together with Ján Francisci-Rimavský, drafted the *Memorandum Slovenského národa* (The Memorandum of the Slovak Nation) in 1861, and clerics like Msgr. Andrej Hlinka, the co-founder of the „Slovak People's Party", staunchly stood up to be counted, in the face of continuous Hungarian oppression and denigration, only to suffer harassment and imprisonment for daring to champion the cause of their people. The American Revolution of 1776 had given new impetus to the concept that „all men are created equal" causing many of Europe's old guard to pause and shake their heads, but nonetheless to take note of the sweeping changes in how mankind in general perceived itself in the New World, and certainly in the Old World as well. It was the French Revolution

---

[22] Also the birthplace of one of this century's most noted Slovaks, Alexander Dubček.

of 1789, and the ensuing Napoleonic wars, which spread the ideals of „*liberty, fraternity and equality*" among the mainstream populations of the European kingdoms. The motivation provided by these „novel" innovations, helped to lay the groundwork for the Pan-Slavic Movement of the 1800s, which by stressing the cultural ties of the western, southern and eastern Slavonic branches which formed and still constitute Europe's largest ethnic group,

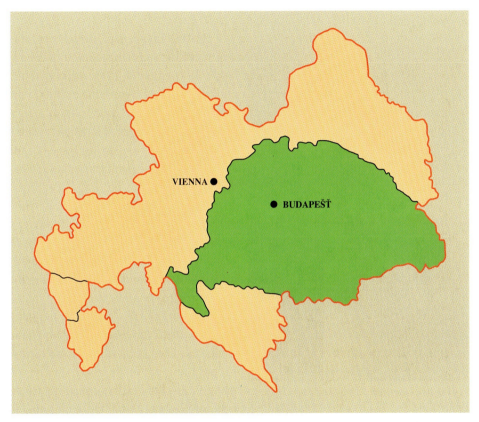

Austria and Hungary 1796 – 1918. Map courtesy of the Matica Slovenská

sought to stem the tide of assimilation that appeared to be engulfing the Slovaks, Moravians, Czechs, Slovenians, Rusins, Croatians and other of the Slavic nations not so numerically populous as their Polish, Russian and Ukrainian brothers. A paranoid Hungarian government particularly disparaged the movement and did its utmost to prevent the furtherance of any contacts between the Slovaks and their fellow Slavs.

Ján Kollár and Pavol Jozef Šafárik were among the chief Slovak proponents of the Pan-Slavic movement, which though seeking an expansion of cultural links with the other

Slavic nations, did not, *per se*, aim at a political union with them. The Hungarian government preferred to view Pan-Slavism as a direct attack on its hegemony, and sought its destruction. Hungary became so obsessed with the fear of a „Slavist behind every rock" mentality, that every imaginable ill and evil was laid at the door of the Pan-Slavist movement by her. To quote Ľudovít Štúr, „*Every undertaking, on however a small scale, to promote enlightenment and well-being, and to prevent the rights of the Slav nations from being forgotten, was decried as Pan-Slavism.*"[23]

Monument to Ľudovít Štúr in the town of Modra, where he died on January 12, 1856. Photograph courtesy of the Matica Slovenská

In 1848 Europe was gripped by a series of nationalistic uprisings, generally referred to as the Revolution of 1848, the underlying causes of which were both political and economic. A „Magyarized" Slovak, Lajos Kossuth led the Magyar Revolutionary forces to victory against against the forces of the Austrian empire, whose reigning monarch was the Habsburg emperor, Ferdinand I (V), which resulted in the granting of a new constitution to Hungary. Yet, while savoring their own new found freedoms, the Hungarians strove diligently to deny the same rights they had achieved to the Slovaks, Croatians and the other ethnic groups under their sway.

So, on May 10, 1848, Štúr and other Slovak leaders addressed a petition to the Hungarian Diet, requesting for the Slovak nation: Universal suffrage; Freedom of the press; Freedom of assembly and association; a Slovak National Guard; the Introduction of the Slovak language into grammar and secondary schools, as well as into seminaries and teachers' schools, and the formation of a Slovak university; a General parliament for all the nations of the multinational Hungarian kingdom, with the right of each deputy to use his native language; Provincial assemblies based on ethnicity and the right to use one's native language in public and in the courts of the land. The Hungarian government's reply was its calculated total disregard of the petition. Already in March, the Croatians had asserted their rights by electing General Josip Jelačič to the

---

[23] Yurchak, p. 120.

Painting of the National Assemblage in Turčiansky Svätý Martin in 1861. Picture courtesy of the Matica Slovenská

Ľudovít Štúr (1815 – 1856). Painting by Ivan Pavlisko

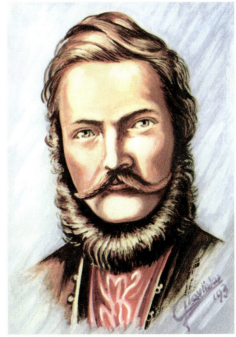

banship of Croatia, without requesting his confirmation by either Budapest or Vienna. On May 13, Serbia followed suit, and installed Stevan Supljikač as the Ban of Serbia.

Then on May 31, 1848 representatives from throughout the Slavic world converged on the city of Prague, in Bohemia, for a great Pan-Slav Congress. Vienna for the most part looked upon the Congress as a buffer to Prussia's push for a Greater Germany, at the expense of Austria. Hungary, on the other hand, viewed it as an attempt by her Slavonic subjects to push for the rights she had consistently denied them, and reserved only for Magyar citizenry.

On June 12th, during the course of the congress, held in an atmosphere bursting with passion and emotion a group of Slavic students clashed in a confrontation with some imperial guard units. The Austrian general, Prince Alfred Windischgrätz declared martial law, and the Slavic Congress was dispersed. Although from the congress itself nothing of note was accomplished, the die had now been cast for rebellion.

The Slovaks having no representation in the Hungarian Diet whatsoever, Jozef Miloslav Hurban made his way to Croatia to plead Slovakia's cause there, at the newly convoked Croatian parliament in Zagreb. There he described the plight of the Slovak nation under the Magyars as being comparable to the proverbial mistreatment of Christians under the Turkish sultanate. The Croatians embraced the Slovak cause and their Ban, General Jelačič sent Budapest the

Monument dedicated to Viliam Šulek and Karol Holuby, on the outskirts of the village of Šulekovo in the County of Hlohovec, raised in 1928. Photograph by Alexander Psica

message, *„With sword in hand we shall prove the times are past when one nation may presume to rule over another."*[24] Magyar rights were one thing, but the audacity of the Slovaks and the Croatians to demand theirs, was quite another. The seeds of the Revolution of 1848 had also firmly taken root among the oppressed peoples under Magyar jurisdiction, and the Hungarians were especially incensed that the soldiery of Slovak extraction refused to raise arms for the Magyars against the likewise rebellious Croatians and Serbs.

---

[24] Capek, p. 78.

Štefan Moyses (1797 – 1869), Roman Catholic Bishop of Banská Bystrica, the first President of the Matica Slovenská. Picture courtesy of the Matica Slovenská

Pavol Országh Hviezdoslav (1849 – 1921), Slovakia's Poet Laureate. Picture courtesy of the Matica Slovenská

Hungarian revenge against Slovak revolutionary insurgents was swift and deliberate. Rough scaffolds, the so-called „Kossuth gallows", named for the arch-magyarophile Lajos Kossuth, were erected along the highways and byways of Slovakia. The gibbets were called „liberty trees" in scornful mockery of the fact, that only death brought liberty to the Slovaks from Budapest; numbers of Slovak leaders and potential leaders exited this life on them.

Through the efforts and under the leadership of Jozef Miloslav Hurban a Slovak National Council was established and a 500 plus volunteer army created. On September 19, Hurban's force of amateur troops entered Slovakia in the vicinity of the town of Myjava and were quartered in Brezová. Hundreds of daily new arrivals helped to swell the forces of this patriotic, though ill-equipped and ill-trained band of irregular soldiery. Although it enjoyed a few minor successes in encounters with some units of the Hungarian army during the period of September 20 through 27, it was the much superior Hungarian army sent against them by Budapest that claimed victory on September 28, 1848. The survivors fell back into Moravia and were disbanded there.

The sacrifice of two of the many youthful Slovak heroes who participated in the 1848 – 1849 Slovak Uprising is commemorated today by a memorial in the village of Šulekovo (now named for one of the young Slovak martyrs who so willingly gave up his life for his country) on the outskirts of the town of Hlohovec. It marks the spot where, on October 26, 1848, two Slovak students, Viliam Šulek and Karol Holuby, of the Slovak Volunteer Army were executed by hanging after having been captured by the Magyars as they tried to return home after the defeat near Brezová.

Also in October of 1848, an anti-imperial revolt swept through Vienna. The Hungarians gave their backing to the rebellious forces and sent help to assist them. However, it was not long before the imperial forces, under Prince Windischgrätz's command, routed the Viennese revolutionaries and their Hungarian allies and put down the insurrection. Taking the matter a step further, General Windischgrätz decided to stamp out the newly won Hungarian gains and restore the status quo. Knowing full well that they could never expect any concessions from the Hungarian government, except that of „the right to die on a liberty tree", the Slovak leaders under Hurban and Štúr gave their support to the Austrian emperor, in hopes that he would champion their cause.

A new volunteer army was formed, and during the autumn the Slovak forces achieved some notable successes, including the occupation of all the northern Slovak counties, as well as the capture of the town of Žilina. In the meantime, General Windischgrätz's forces had cleared out whatever Hungarian army units still remained behind in Slovakia. The Austrians and the Magyars relentlessly continued their fight locked in a deadly power struggle from which neither side would retreat an inch. On the 7th of March, the Austrian emperor voided the previous year's accommodations to the Hungarians and issued the

Magyars a new constitution. Hoping for imperial support in their quest for Slovakia to be named an Austrian crown land, and thus removed from the direct rule of Hungary, a Slovak delegation met with the new emperor, Francis Joseph I, in the Moravian town of Olomouc on March 20, 1849. Though well received by his Imperial Highness, nothing of substance was promised. Shortly afterwards, the Austrian government snuffed out whatever hopes may have existed towards that end, by declaring that Slovakia's status would only be decided upon after the restoration of imperial power and law in Hungary as well as in Slovakia.

Some months later, the Hungarian government was brought to its knees when the army of the Russian tsar Nicholas I, under the command of General Prince Ivan Feodorovič Paškievič, intervened on behalf of the Austrians and invaded Hungary. In a much too little, much too late scenario, the Hungarian Diet passed a law promising its oppressed non-Magyar subjects a chance at equality, in exchange for their now coming to preserve Hungarian dominion. Faced with the task of going it alone against the might of Austria and Russia, amidst the alienation of the non-Magyar peoples of the kingdom, which the Magyars had brought on themselves, Hungary capitulated to a victorious Austria. On August 13, 1849, the Magyar army command surrendered to the Russians at Világos, and the Revolution as well as the Slovak Uprising of 1848 – 1849 were over.

In the wake of the aftermath of the Slovak Uprising of 1848 – 1849, although Slovakia's position for the most part remained unchanged, the uprising, in and of itself, showed that the Slovak nation was willing to take up arms to fight for its rights, even though it lacked the military training and equipment sorely needed for such an endeavor. The Austrian Government had promised nothing and had given nothing. And from the Hungarian side, Magyarization became even more stringently pursued.

The years passed as Slovakia's unchanged status weathered the harsh Magyarization policies with which Budapest sought to exterminate the culture, history and language of the Slovaks. The decree of March 7, 1849 that supposedly guaranteed equality to all the peoples residing within the borders of the Hungarian dominions, did not specifically name the Slovak nation, and so under Hungarian law was not considered to apply to them. The years of Magyar absolutism continued on as ever before. And still for the Slovaks there was no representation in the Hungarian Diet.

On June 6, 1861, in the face of Magyar threats of imprisonment or worse, some 6,000 Slovak leaders and patriots, from various walks of life and from the length and breadth of Slovakia, rallied in the town of Turčiansky Svätý Martin in a show of national solidarity against the injustices of the Hungarian government. The assemblage resulted in Štefan Marko Daxner's and Ján Francisci-Rimavský's drafting of *The Memorandum of the Slovak Nation*. This document gave voice to the demands of the Slovak nation in the spheres of political, educational and religious life within the Hungarian state. A summation of those demands was incorporated into their motto of „*A one, free constitutional country, and in it liberty, equality and fraternity of nations*". Unfortunately, but with the usual turn of events marking Slovak-Hungarian relations, that document when presented by Ján Francisci-Rimavský to the vice-president of the Hungarian Diet, Kálmán Tisza, who promised not only to submit it, but to promote the Memorandum's demands in parliament, was deftly put aside. Kálmán Tisza's words had been empty and deceptive. Neither the presentation nor the promotion of the Memorandum ever materialized.

All attempts to gain any concessions for Slovakia and the Slovaks from the Hungarian Diet were frustrated time and time again. One outstanding achievement was, however, finally accomplished sometime after the June 6th assembly in Turčiansky Svätý Martin. After many deliberate postponements by the Hungarian parliament, covering the years 1851 to 1863, the Slovaks, with the approbation of the Austrian Emperor Francis Joseph, and despite Magyar opposition, opened a cultural institute. Thus after extremely difficult „externally" caused labor pains, the birth of Slovakia's hallowed institution known as the Matica Slovenská took place on May 31, 1863. It is interesting to note that the life of the Matica Slovenská began in the same year marking the 1000th anniversary of the arrival of the saintly Thessalonian Brothers, Constantine-Cyril and Methodius in the land of the Slovaks, from Constantinople, to preach the gospel of Christ. The opening of Slovakia's premier cultural association and repository was met by the Slovak people with rejoicing and celebration. The Roman Catholic Bishop of Banská Bystrica, Štefan Moyses, often referred to as the „*Father of the Slovak people*" presided over the occasion, as the first president of the Matica Slovenská.

The cultural life of Slovakia, still viewed apprehensively and contemptuously by the Hungarian government, at last had a focal point in the Matica Slovenská. The financial task of its maintenance, and that of the few Slovak educational institutions that were now allowed to come into being, rested on the unstinting support of the Slovak people at large. And although the Emperor Francis Joseph had graciously contributed 1000 florins towards the founding of the Matica Slovenská, it was, for the most part, the Slovak people themselves who shouldered the costs of its construction and upkeep. From Budapest nothing was given, and needless to say, nothing was expected.

Yet, for all practical purposes it was the heavy hand of their Hungarian rulers that determined the daily lives of their Slovak subjects. The struggle for Magyar rights within the empire was at last resolved by the *Ausgleich* of 1867 which created the dual monarchy of Austria-Hungaria. The non-Magyar inhabitants of the kingdom of Hungary were now left to the „tender mercies" of Budapest, which increased its efforts a hundredfold to assimilate and denationalize the Slovak nation. From 1868 on, all activities of a decidedly Slovak nature were considered treasonous and their suppression became a main priority of

Budapest. It wasn't long before Slovak educational institutions were shuttered and publishers run out of business with ruinous taxes imposed on them by the Hungarian government. And then on April 13, 1875, the hard-earned capital and property of the Matica Slovenská itself were confiscated and its doors closed.[25]

The remaining years of the century saw most of Slovakia's leadership subjected to whatever kinds of trials and tribulations could be placed in their way by Budapest. The use of the Slovak language in all public places was viewed as paramount to treason and anti-Hungarian. Slovak placenames, that were centuries old, were Magyarized, not to mention the Magyarization of thousands of original Slovak family names.

The view of many Hungarian nationalists of the era can be epitomized by the following pronouncement of Magyar extremists: „*Tót nem ember/A Slovak is not a human being*",[26] while Hungarian prime ministers, such as Július Andrássy and Kálmán Tisza, spewed forth their venomous views that, „*Rather than give political and national rights to the Slovaks, we will murder and massacre them to the last man,*"[27] and calumniously proclaimed, „*There is no Slovak nation.*"[28]

The Magyar-Hungarian solution to the Slovaks living in their „shared" kingdom was simple – exterminate them, or to use the current expression – they would have to be „ethnically cleansed". The advocation of what may be termed the „Magyar State-idea" doctrine, which was pursued by the Hungarian government and promulgated by such a well-placed Hungarian government official as Béla Grünwald in his brochure „*A Felvidék*", was clearly stated by the American writer Thomas Capek, „*To rule was the destiny of the Magyars; to follow must be the mission of the rest. Danger to the state lurked in the national awakening of the Slovaks, Servians (sic) and others, and this awakening should be promptly suppressed. A native of Hungary could not be a patriot unless he endorsed in full the Magyar state idea. While it might be permissible, reasoned Grünwald for a peasant or laborer to converse, for example in Slovak, a cultured person, reared on Hungarian soil, should under no circumstances speak, think, or feel, except as a Magyar. A Slovak of education who remained true to his ancestry was deficient in patriotism and a traitor to his country* (read: country = the Hungarian government). *To Magyarize Slovakland was the government's manifest duty, and it should be effected by forcible means if necessary.*" The summary

---

[25] Forty-four years after the Hungarian Ministry of Interior Affairs had ordered it closed, the Matica Slovenská was finally reopened in 1919 after the creation of the first Czecho-Slovak Republic; its first General Assembly being held on August 25 of that year. Today it holds the exalted position of being Slovakia's national and premier cultural repository and historical archive.
[26] Yurchak, p. 153. Palickar, p. 254.
[27] Palickar, p. 253.
[28] Yurchak, p. 149. Oddo, p. 140. Marko and Martinický, p. 9.

of Grünwald's work ends with, „*There was no Slovak nation, only a horde speaking that language. The so-called Slovak party consisted of a few rebels, who should be done away with; the peasants could then be easily subdued with ease. To the Magyars was allotted the task of exterminating the Slavs living on Hungarian soil. A compromise with the Slovaks was impossible. There was only one expedient left – to wipe them out. If the Magyars wished to live, they must increase their numbers by assimilating the non-Magyar people.*"[29]

Grünwald further stated that „*In Upper Hungary* (read: Slovakia) *secondary schools are like machines into which Slovak boys are loaded on one end to leave as Magyars on the other end.*"[30]

After having read Béla Grünwald's work, at the urgent behest of several Hungarian-Magyars, the well-known English historian, R. W. Seton-Watson's succinct comment, on Grünwald's Hungarian supremacy diatribe, sums it up best. „*My anger and astonishment were boundless. I learned, that this book, so often praised to me, was of unusually worthless value; one of the very worst books it has ever been necessary for me to read in my work. I needed to exercise great self-restraint to read it to the end. The Magyars should be thankful that its shameless revelations have never been translated in to a western tongue.*"[31]

As the nineteenth century, that so auspiciously had witnessed such an unfolding of Slovak literary and intellectual life, now came to a close, a still downtrodden Slovakia staggered under the heavy yoke of Hungarian oppression, as she struggled to preserve and maintain her national identity in the face of almost insurmountable odds. Dark clouds had obscured the brightness of Slovakia's new day, but the hopes, and dreams, of a radiant new dawn still lay beyond the horizon.

---

[29] Capek, p. 96.
[30] Marko and Martinický, p. 9.
[31] Yurchak, p. 153.

CHAPTER SIX

The Twentieth Century
The End and The Beginning

Hungarian absolutism and enforced Magyarization were still the crook and flail that represented Budapest's rule of the Slovaks as the twentieth century dawned.

In the elections of 1901, the Slovaks had gained a foothold in the Hungarian Diet, by capturing two parliamentary seats in that body. In the 1905 elections that figure was increased by two more, to four. Still, these numbers, although at last giving the Slovak people a voice in the national assembly of the Hungarian state, were nothing more than a mere drop in the bucket. In response to the harsh realities of life for the Slovaks under the dictates of Budapest, in 1905, a young Roman Catholic priest Andrej Hlinka took up the cause of his people and co-founded, together with František Skyčák, the Slovak People's Party. Their avowed goal was to gain for the Slovak nation the rights they had heretofore been denied by their Magyar-Hungarian rulers. In 1906, trying to achieve their goals, by way of the system, the Slovaks under the direction of Hlinka and other Slovak leaders, had gained seven seats in the Hungarian National Assembly. Still Hungary's adamant and unbending will prevailed against the granting of any concessions to the Slovaks.

In 1907, the Apponyi Law, named for the Hungarian Minister of Education Albert Apponyi, was passed by the Hungarian parliament. This law forbade the operation of all but Magyar schools within the Hungarian kingdom and further required a specific oath of loyalty to the Magyar government from each and every private and public school teacher. Instructors were also punished if their charges were not instructed in the Magyar language. The protesting voices of the Slovak representatives in the Hungarian Diet were to no avail as they drowned in a sea of Magyar accord for the law's enactment.

For having had the audacity to champion the rights and cause of his people, Andrej Hlinka was especially singled out to bear the displeasure of the Hungarian powers-that-were. His endeavors and tireless efforts on the campaign trail to promote Slovak parliamentary candidates, and successfully so, had made him a man marked for retribution by the Magyars. Through the machinations of the Hungarian government a charge of simony was now leveled against him by his direct superior, the Hungarian bishop of Spiš, Alexander Párvy, who suspended Hlinka from performing any of his priestly duties. Having thus sought to disgrace Hlinka in the eyes of the faithful, and his flock, the Hungarian government now brought secular charges against him under the „catch-all" law aimed at decimating any but Magyar nationalism, that forbade „incitement against the Magyar nationality."

Against Magyarone, that is pro-Magyar, priests who had likewise actively campaigned in the elections, but on behalf of the Hungarian government's candidates, no charges at all were pressed by either the Hungarian religious or secular authorities. Adding to the tensions of the moment, Hlinka, who had been actively involved for several years, in the soliciting of funds to help build a church in his home-village of Černová, was now forbidden by Bishop Párvy to participate in the consecration of the now completed church. Hoping that their pastor and Černová's native son would participate in their church's dedication, the people pleaded with Párvy so that its dedication might be delayed. As yet the Roman Curia had not ruled on the accusation of simony. Ignoring their pleas, Párvy scheduled the dedication for October 27, 1907. On that date, one of Alexander Párvy's Magyarone priests, together with a Hungarian civil servant, as well as the Magyar police entered the little Liptov village to accomplish Párvy's directive. Met enroute by the Černová villagers who again pleaded for a postponement, amid flaring tempers, the Hungarians, without warning, fired on the unarmed Slovak protestors. When the smoke had cleared, nine Slovak villagers lay dead; another sixty plus lay wounded, of these six died later. The church of Černová had at last been consecrated... with Slovak blood. Although fully acquitted by Rome of the simony charge, Hlinka was now convicted by the Hungarian government under their „catch-all" law and incarcerated as a political prisoner by the Magyars in the Hungarian town of Szeged. In March of 1908, fifty-nine survivors of the infamous Černová Massacre were sentenced to various prison terms. Unfortunately, it took the bloodbath at Černová to bring the plight of the Slovak nation to center stage before the international community. In a few short years, however, Slovakia's fight for her rights would be interrupted by World War I. Waged from 1914 to 1918 and called the „*war to end all wars*", it unfortunately did not do so!

Not only in Slovakia, but all across Europe the currents of change had inexorably been running in torrents, and in the space of four short year the winds of World War I would sweep away the ascendancy of what had been the old order, and usher in a new era. Slovakia having endured Hungarian dominion, for almost a thousand years, would heartily welcome the extrication of her bondage from the yoke of the Magyars, which the war brought about. With a joyous feeling of deliverance and liberation, she would pledge herself to a union proposed by the neighboring land of Bohemia, with the assumption that she would be granted an equal and autonomous relationship in the new post-war federation. Andrej

The Massacre in Černová. Painting by M. Kuniak. Photograph by František Šlachta

Hlinka (who again would be called upon to raise his voice for Slovakia's rights within the Czecho-Slovak framework) and General Milan Rastislav Štefánik were among those Slovak leaders who, at the outset, worked towards the Slovak-Czech partnership which would produce a new entity to be called Czecho-hyphen-Slovakia.

Milan Rastislav Štefánik, the son of a Lutheran minister, was born in the village of Košariská, in Nitra County, on July 21, 1880. He was for the most part educated abroad, became an astronomer, a pilot, a naturalized French citizen and a Brigadier General in the French military, through it all maintaining a love for the land of his birth that never diminished. His friendship with a number of distinguished French and Italian nationals gained him and by extension Slovakia, many friends in the international community of the times. Having been approached by the Czech leaders, Tomáš Garrigue Masaryk, a former professor of his, and Edvard Beneš, during the war years to participate in the construction of a postwar state to be called the Czecho-Slovak Republic, and which would include the countries of Slovakia, Moravia, Bohemia and later Ruthenia,[32] Štefánik acceded, and became an integral part of the Štefánik, Masaryk and Beneš triumvirate. By October of 1918 however, Štefánik, it is believed had begun to have misgivings about the similarity of his goals and those of Masaryk and Beneš and was becoming disillusioned with unfolding events. As the war began heading towards its climax, the Czech Revolutionary National Committee announced, on October 28, 1918, its assumption of the governing of the Czech lands. Two days later, the Slovak National Council announced its intention of joining with Bohemia

Czecho-Slovakia 1918 – 1938. Map courtesy of the Matica Slovenská

and Moravia to form Czecho-Slovakia. And then on November 11, 1918, World War I officially ended.

In December of 1918, Masaryk returned to Prague to assume the provisional leadership of a republic that most Slovaks believed was to be an equally partnered Czecho-Slovak federation. General Štefánik, in the meantime, had gone to the Far East and Siberia to attend to matters concerning the Czecho-Slovak legions posted there. In January 1919, he returned to France and in April to Italy, from where he had decided to return by plane to Bratislava. On May 4, 1919, as his plane was approaching to land, it burst into flames and crashed at Ivanka pri Dunaji, outside the Slovak capital. General Štefánik and his two

---

[32] The Ruthenian representatives in fact issued a ‚Declaration of Union' with the new Czecho-Slovakia on May 8, 1919. See R. Seton-Watson, *A History of the Czechs and Slovaks* (Hamden: Archon Books, 1965) p. 234.

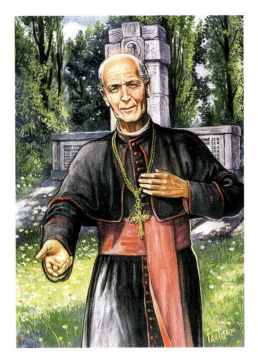

Msgr. Andrej Hlinka (1864 – 1938). Painting by Ivan Pavlisko

Msgr. Jozef Tiso, the President of the First Slovak Republic. Painting by Ivan Pavlisko

Italian co-pilots died instantly.[33] Slovakia had lost a beloved son and another champion of her rights.

In terms of nationalism, the aspirations of Slovak nationalists were, and are, basically no different than those of the Irish, Israelis, Croatians, Palestinians, Hungarians, Czechs, Polish and a host of other nations who desired to be governed along their own ethnic lines, in accordance with their own historic traditions. As much as the terms „Czechoslovak", „the Czechoslovak language" and „the Czechoslovak nation" were thrown around, no such people, language or nation existed, or have ever existed.

The British historian, C. A. Macartney, poignantly, took to task and denounced the advocation of Prague's errant policy of ‚Czechoslovakism' as follows. „*In a more general way, the Czechs have done much to arouse the resentment, even of Slovaks naturally favorable toward them, and have grievously damaged their own cause, by overstressing the ‚Czechoslovak' idea and by certain measures regarded by the Slovaks as attempts to deprive them of their own nationality. It is paradoxical, but natural, that the weakness of the foundations on which the ‚Czechoslovak' idea rested became most apparent the moment that the idea received official recognition. Such phrases as ‚Czechoslovak nationality' and ‚Czechoslovak language' might be used for the benefit of the outside world, and in constitutional and other State documents, but the fact remains that to the vast majority of both peoples the idea remained a pure fiction, and the languages, like the peoples, were, in, solid fact, two and not one. The practical solution was to use both languages on an equal footing in matters of common concern, while giving Czech priority in the western half of the Republic and Slovak in the east. In fact however, Czech was employed almost*

Gen. Milan Rastislav Štefánik (1880 – 1919). Painting by Ivan Pavlisko

---

[33] Although several theories have been bandied about as to the cause of that fatal explosion, to this day a view held by many Slovaks, whether rightfully or wrongfully, is the belief that a plot was masterminded in Prague to be rid of Štefánik whose views and those of certain Czech leaders had begun to diverge; and who, because of his immense popularity, was definitely a great potential threat to Beneš' goal of becoming the next president of Czecho-Slovakia after Masaryk.

The Great Cathedral of Bratislava, dedicated to St. Martin of Tours and the city's royal castle dominate Bratislava's skyline. An ancient tradition holds that Conchessa, the mother of St. Patrick (389 – 461 A.D.), Ireland's national patron saint was the niece of the Roman or quite possibly Romano-Slavic, St. Martin. Photograph by Dagmar Veliká

Interior of St. Martin's Cathedral. The cathedral church originally stood on castle hill in Bratislava and was called the Church of the Holy Saviour. In 1221 A. D., its site was transferred to what is today the city's Staré Mesto or Old Town. In the 14th century it was rebuilt and renamed for St. Martin. Photograph courtesy of the Archdiocese of Bratislava–Trnava

exclusively in Bohemia, and a great many of the Czech officials and teachers in Slovakia thought that the problem of the existing duality could most easily be solved by eliminating Slovak as a literary language altogether. Much of the teaching in the new schools, up to and including the University, was carried out in Czech, not all the teachers troubling to make themselves acquainted with the language of their pupils. Much resentment was aroused by the methods in this respect of Czech professors at Bratislava University, who should, it was felt, have taken the lead in fostering and developing the Slovak national language and culture, whereas they worked actively, on the contrary, to destroy it."[34]

One of Czecho-Slovakia's main problems was that, like the former Austro-Hungarian empire, it was an artificial state composed of not one people or one nation, but a multinational state made up of four units – Slovakia, Moravia, Bohemia and Ruthenia, along with some significant numbers of other ethnic groups within the Czecho-Slovak territorial borders, most notably the Germans in Bohemia and Hungarians in Slovakia. This multinational re-grouping of nations, in what might be called a mini-copy of the former Austria-Hungaria, without again the neutralizing factor of an „official" state language that was not the native language of any of the state's inhabitants, such as Latin had been in the old medieval Hungarian kingdom, or the English language of a now ethnic American minority in the United States, condemned history to repeat itself. Once again, one nation would promote its language and traditions over the others and, Prague, being the new national capital, that language and those traditions would be Czech and the new governmental policy – centralism; translating to a concentration of control and power

The capital city of Slovakia personified as Bratislava Regina Istropolitana – Bratislava, Queen of the Danube. Oil Painting by Mikuláš Klimčák. Courtesy of the artist

---

[34] C. A. Macartney, *Hungary and Her Successors 1919 – 1937* (London: Oxford University Press, 1965) pp. 126 – 127.

in Prague. In such a system there was no room for the historic Slovak aspirations of autonomy and self-government. Prague would govern and the other peoples would acquiesce. The promises made beforehand to gain Slovakia's entry into the union, by guaranteeing her autonomy, were swept aside as nothing more than empty words on a piece of paper by none other than Czech president, Masaryk himself. Once again Slovakia had been given a hard lesson, teaching her that self-government is the best government. Slovak federalism was made to bow to Czech centralism.

Adding to the discontent of the majority of Slovaks concerning the abandoned Pittsburgh Agreement of May 30, 1918, which had supported Slovakia's autonomy, that Masaryk had signed and then renounced, was the land exchange between Prague and Warsaw,

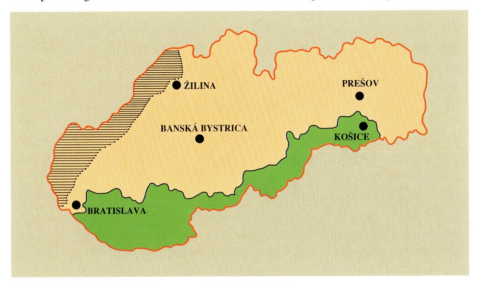

First Slovak Republic 1939 – 1945. Map courtesy of the Matica Slovenská

that gave parts of Slovakia's Orava and Spiš regions to Poland in return for the acquisition of part of the the coal rich Cieszyn area that bordered the Czech lands and now became a part of them under the name Český Těšín. Again Slovakia had lost out by her membership in the Czecho-Slovak state.

As the years progressed, Slovakia's civil service that in the beginning had needed and so had been filled by Czech bureaucrats, continued for the most part to remain so. The newly-educated Slovak civil servants, however, remained on the sidelines, largely unemployed and stagnating in their own land. Discontent with the Czecho-Slovak union in Slovakia continued to mount and seethe. Feelings of animosity towards the Czechs who, more often than not, exhibited an attitude of superiority and condescension in their dealings with the Slovaks, continued to rise as more and more Slovaks began to feel like second-class citizens once again in their own homeland. Slovaks began to see Slovakia, not as a partner in the Czecho-Slovak experience, but as a colonial possession of Prague. It is only fair to state that animosity existed in both the Slovak and the Czech camps. The Czech view was that Slovakia and the Slovaks should be unremittingly grateful for whatever the Czechs had done for them and by extension be dutifully governable in the process.

By the 1930s, the tensions had given rise to a feeling in Slovakia that the union of the Slovaks and Czechs was for all practical purposes over and that the Slovaks should go their own separate way. The rise of Adolph Hitler to power in Nazi Germany provided the solution, unsought as it was. Hitler wanted the Sudetenland, which was now also part of the Czech lands and ran along the German-Czech border of Czechoslovakia. And thus to gain what the Nazis referred to as *lebensraum* (living space), Hitler decided on the dissolution of Czecho-Slovakia. Czechia and Moravia were to become German Protectorates, and Slovakia, if she refused to declare independence under the aegis of Nazi Germany, was to be partitioned among her neighbors. As for the reaction of the main European allies of Czecho-Slovakia to Hitler's plans, England, in effect, by the Munich Pact, threw Czecho-Slovakia as a sop to the „dogs of war", while France looked the other way.

Jozef Tiso, a Catholic priest, now became the President of the first Slovak Republic. Myriad questions have been asked and many still remain to be addressed and answered from this period. Questions leap forth begging answers, not the least of which concern the terrible Jewish deportations to the Nazi death camps. The memories of the brutalities of the Second World War are still fresh and painful to a great many people. With the Allied defeat of the Axis powers, President Tiso was turned over to Edvard Beneš, president of the re-instated Czechoslovak government. Upon the Slovak President's arrival in Prague, Bohumil Ečer, the head of Beneš' War Crimes Commission had him shackled as he declared, „*Here I have independent Slovakia bound in chains.*"[35] At the Prague government's instigation, Tiso was tried, convicted and executed by hanging on April 18, 1947, and then secretly buried on orders from Hradčany.

By the end of 1948, the communists had completed their takeover of Czechoslovakia and, with a mighty thud the iron curtain had fallen, splitting Europe into two newly demarcated camps, called East and West. The phrase Central Europe was now stricken from the vocabulary of the new „us and them" era of the Cold War.

Democracy and religion were repressed. The new dogma was communism, and those who didn't agree with its tenets or propagators, soon learned to keep their thoughts to

---

[35] Oddo, p. 311, Konštantín Čulen, *Po Svätoplukovi druhá naša hlava – Život Dr. Jozefa Tisu* (Middletown: Jednota Printery, 1947) pp. 385 – 386.

themselves, or else suffer imprisonment or death. Churches, monasteries and convents were suppressed and their material goods confiscated. Priests, ministers, nuns and other religious were arrested, given mock trials and for the most part sent to labor camps. Private enterprise was halted and disbanded; any and all opposition to the regime was looked on as treasonous and persecuted. Democracy was fettered and Communism reigned supreme. Its goal was „to bury the capitalist West" and all who stood in its way.

And so life continued on, as best it could, under the harsh and repressive totalitarian regimes that governed from Prague, by the grace of Red Moscow, in what was now called the Czechoslovak Socialist Republic. Life under the inflexible measures of the new communist controlled dictatorship system, left little time for the past worries of a former life to be contemplated.

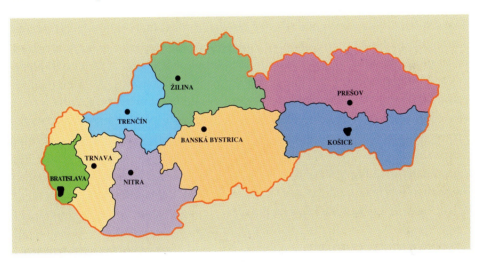

The Slovak Republic from 1993. Map courtesy of the Matica Slovenská

No thaw would come until 1968, when the first Slovak to hold the position of First Party Secretary of the Czechoslovak Communist Party, a Moscow apparatchik named Alexander Dubček would promote a limited democracy referred to as „Socialism with a human face." Alarmed Moscow sent the troops of the Warsaw Pact to crush what came to be termed the „Czecho-Slovak Spring". The invasion of Czecho-Slovakia on August 20, 1968 ended its flirtation with democracy. When the dust had settled, the country was occupied. More than 250 Soviet T-54 tanks alone had been sped across the Hungarian border just to take Slovakia's capital city of Bratislava. If life in the police state had been bad before, it suddenly got even worse. For many Slovaks, it seemed that even hope had escaped this time from Pandora's box, and now nothing at all was left to comfort them at this time of loss. The wheels of daily life ground on as ever before, only now under the ever more watchful eye of the Communist party.

It would be almost another twenty-five years before the last troops of the Warsaw Pact armies that came to occupy Slovakia would finally leave. And that, only with the surprise collapse of Soviet Communism under Mikhail Gorbachev. Now that the tanks and planes and guns of the Russian military were no longer available to prop up the puppet governments of Moscow's old communist rulers, one by one the former countries of the Soviet Bloc declared for independence. And in November of 1989, the „Velvet Revolution", so-called because of its lack of bloodshed, swept through Czecho-Slovakia, and democracy was re-born.

Her aspirations and objectives having been continuously frustrated, and never really fulfilled, within the confines of the Czechoslovak state by laws and rulers not of her choosing, Slovakia seized, once again, the reins of her own destiny. In 1992, she proclaimed her sovereignty and drafted a new constitution. And then amidst the general rejoicing and exultation of her people, on January 1, 1993, she declared herself independent of the Czecho-Slovak union, and established herself as a member of the family of nations, as a reborn and resurgent nation and country – the Slovak Republic! A new dawn had broken which heralded the promise of a bright new future. And as church bells chimed and pealed, in the presence of Slovakia's new Premier Vladimír Mečiar, his cabinet, their families and as many of the citizens of the newly independent Slovakia as could fill the spaces of the great church, Slovakia's first Metropolitan since the days of Saint Methodius, Archbishop Ján Sokol of Bratislava-Trnava, gratefully intoned a solemn *Te Deum* in the great Co-Cathedral of St. Martin in Bratislava. Freedom had, at last, found its way back into the lives of *the People of the Word*.

The Municipal Coat-of-Arms of Bratislava. Courtesy of the Matica Slovenská

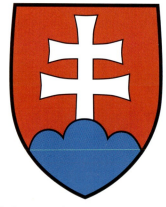

The State Coat-of-Arms of Slovakia. Courtesy of the Matica Slovenská

Chronology of Historical Events

4th/5th Centuries Migration of the proto-Slovaks
623 Beginning of the reign of Samo
631 Battle of Vogastisburg, Samo defeats King Dagobert
658 Death of Samo
799 Charlemagne defeats the Avars
828 Adalram, Archbishop of Salzburg consecrates Prince Pribina's church in Nitra
833 Formation of the Nitrian-Moravian State, beginnings of the Great Moravian Empire
846 Rastislav becomes Prince of the Slovieni (Slovaks)
847 Pribina becomes Prince of Blatnohrad
855 War between Prince Rastislav and King Louis the German
861 Death of Pribina, succession of his son Prince Koceľ
863 Arrival in Slovakia of Constantine, Methodius and the Byzantine Mission from Constantinople
864 Frankish assault on Devín Castle
867 The Byzantine Mission visits Blatnohrad, Venice and Rome
869 Constantine-Cyril dies in Rome on February 14
870 Rastislav, betrayed by his nephew Svätopluk to the Franks, is blinded and dies; Svätopluk becomes king
871 Svätopluk held captive by Carloman; he wins his release and retakes his crown
874 Treaty of Forchheim signed by King Svätopluk and King Louis the German
880 The kingship of Svätopluk sanctioned in the papal bull *Industriae tuae*; Nitra created the first Slovak and the first Slavic diocese; the Papacy reaffirms the usage of Slavonic for the sacred liturgy
885 Death of Methodius, Papal Legate and Archbishop of Great Moravia and Pannonia, on April 6

894 Death of Svätopluk I
895 Defection of the Czech tribes from Svätopluk's empire
896 The Magyars cross the Tisa River and enter Slovakia
907 Battle of Bratislava, destruction of the Great Moravian Empire on or about July 4
955 Otto I of Germany defeats the Magyars at the Battle of the Lechfeld
1031 Slovakia incorporated into the kingdom of Hungary
1241 Invasion of Batu Khan and the Tatars
1301 Andrew the III, the last of the Arpád dynasty dies
1312 Battle of Rozhanovce – June 15, defeat of the forces of Matúš Čak Trenčiansky by Charles Robert of Anjou
1439 The death of Albert of Habsburg sparks the War of Succession
1453 The Fall of Constantinople – May 28
1465 King Matthias Corvinus establishes the first university in Bratislava
1517 Martin Luther posts his theses on the doors of the Wittenberg castle-church
1526 The Battle of Mohács – August 29; Budapest falls to the Turks on September 10
1604 – 1711 Insurrections of the great land magnates
1618 – 1648 The Thirty Years War
1663 Turkish assault on Slovakia
1683 Turks defeated at the Battle of Vienna – September 12
1688 Birth of Juraj Jánošík in Terchová
1713 Execution of Jánošík in Liptovský Svätý Mikuláš
1722 The steam engine invented in Banská Štiavnica
1762 World's first Mining Academy founded in Banská Štiavnica
1785 Abolition of serfdom in the Austrian crown lands
1792 Onset of Magyarization; foundation of the Slovak Learned Society
1848 Abolition of serfdom in the lands under Hungarian jurisdiction; petitions of the Slovak nation addressed to the Emperor's cabinet on May 10; Pan-Slavic Congress meets in Prague in Bohemia on May 31
1848 – 1849 The Revolution of 1848 and the Slovak Uprising of 1848 – 1849
1861 The Memorandum of the Slovak Nation drafted in Turčiansky Svätý Martin
1863 Foundation of the Matica Slovenská
1867 Creation of the Austro-Hungarian Dual Monarchy
1875 Closure of the Matica Slovenská and confiscation of its property by the Hungarian-Magyar government
18th/20th Centuries Slovak National Revival or Awakening; period extends from the late 1700s into the early 1900s

1907 Černová Massacre on October 27
1915 The Cleveland Agreement
1918 The Pittsburgh Pact; the Martin Declaration; dissolution of the kingdom of Hungary; the establishment of Czecho-Slovakia
1919 Comenius University founded in Bratislava
1939 The First Slovak Republic
1944 The Slovak National Uprising
1945 The Second Czechoslovak Republic
1968 The Warsaw Pact Invasion of Czechoslovakia
1969 The Declaration of Czecho-Slovak federation
1989 The Velvet Revolution, the collapse of Communism
1992 Proclamation of Slovak sovereignty; dissolution of Czechoslovakia on December 31
1993 Slovakia declares independence on January 1

Rulers of Slovakia

MONARCHIES

Samo's Empire
circa 623 – 658 Samo

Principality of Nitra
circa 820 – 833 Pribina

Great Moravian Empire
833 – 846   Mojmír I
846 – 870   Rastislav

Svätopluk Dynasty
870 – 894   Svätopluk I
870 – 871   Slavomír, interim ruler
during Svätopluk's captivity
894 – 907   Mojmír II
894 – 907   Svätopluk II
894 – 907   Bratslav

The Era of Turmoil
907 – 1031

Multi-ethnic Kingdom of Hungary

Arpád Dynasty
1000 – 1038   Stephen I
1038 – 1041   Peter Orseolo of Venice
1041 – 1044   Samuel Aba
1044 – 1046   Peter Orseolo of Venice
1047 – 1060   Andrew I
1060 – 1063   Belo I
1063 – 1074   Solomon
1074 – 1077   Gejza I
1077 – 1095   Ladislav I
1095 – 1116   Koloman
1116 – 1131   Stephen II
1131 – 1141   Belo II
1141 – 1162   Gejza II
1162 – 1172   Stephen III
1162 – 1163   Ladislav II
1163 – 1163   Stephen IV
1172 – 1196   Belo III
1196 – 1204   Imrich
1204 – 1205   Ladislav III
1205 – 1235   Andrew II
1235 – 1270   Belo IV
1270 – 1272   Stephen V
1272 – 1290   Ladislav IV the Cuman
1290 – 1301   Andrew III of Venice

Collateral Branch
1301 – 1305   Václav-Ladislav of Bohemia
1305 – 1308   Otto of Wittelsbach (Bavaria)

Angevin Dynasty
1308 – 1342 Charles Robert of Anjou – Charles I
1342 – 1382 Ľudovít I
1382 – 1395 Marie of Anjou
1385 – 1386 Charles II of Anjou
1387 – 1437 Sigismund of Luxembourg, husband of Marie of Anjou

Non-dynastic
1437 – 1439 Albert II (IV) of Habsburg
1440 – 1444 Vladislav I Jagiellon of Poland
1446 – 1453 Regency of Ján Hunyady
1452 – 1457 Ladislav V, the Posthumous
1458 – 1490 Matthias I Corvinus
1490 – 1516 Vladislav II Jagiellon
1516 – 1526 Ľudovít II
1526 – 1540 Ján Zápoľský, rival of Ferdinand I

Habsburg Dynasty
1526 – 1564 Ferdinand I
1564 – 1576 Maximilian
1576 – 1608 Rudolf
1608 – 1619 Matthias II
1619 – 1637 Ferdinand II
1637 – 1657 Ferdinand III
1647 – 1654 Ferdinand IV, son and co-ruler of Ferdinand III
1657 – 1705 Leopold I
1705 – 1711 Joseph I
1711 – 1740 Charles III (VI)

Habsburg-Lorraine Dynasty
1740 – 1780 Maria Theresa
1780 – 1790 Joseph II
1790 – 1792 Leopold II
1792 – 1835 Francis I (II)
1835 – 1848 Ferdinand I (V)
1848 – 1867 Francis Joseph

Austro-Hungarian Empire
1867 – 1916 Francis Joseph
1916 – 1918 Charles IV (I)

REPUBLICS

First Czecho-Slovak Republic
Presidents
1918 – 1935 Tomáš G. Masaryk
1935 – 1938 Edvard Beneš

FIRST SLOVAK REPUBLIC
President
1939 – 1945 Jozef Tiso

Second Czechoslovak Republic
Presidents
1945 – 1948 Edvard Beneš

Prime Ministers
1945 – 1945 Jan Šrámek
1945 – 1946 Zdeněk Fierlinger
1946 – 1948 Klement Gottwald

Czechoslovak Socialist Republic

Communist Party First Secretaries
1941 – 1951 Rudolf Slánsky

1948 – 1953 Klement Gottwald
1953 – 1968 Antonín Novotný
1968 – 1969 Alexander Dubček
1969 – 1987 Gustáv Husák
1987 – 1989 Miloš Jakeš
1989 – 1989 Karel Urbánek
1989 – 1990 Ladislav Adamec

Presidents
1949 – 1953 Klement Gottwald
1953 – 1957 Antonín Zápotocký
1957 – 1968 Antonín Novotný
1968 – 1975 Ludvík Svoboda
1975 – 1989 Gustáv Husák

Prime Ministers
1948 – 1953 Antonín Zápotocký
1953 – 1963 Viliam Široký
1963 – 1968 Jozef Lenárt
1968 – 1970 Oldřich Černík
1970 – 1988 Lubomír Štrougal
1988 – 1989 Ladislav Adamec

Czech and Slovak Federal Republic

President
1989 – 1992 Václav Havel

Federal Prime Ministers
1989 – 1990 Marián Čalfa
1992 – 1992 Ján Stráský

Slovak Prime Ministers
1989 – 1990 Milan Čič
1990 – 1991 Vladimír Mečiar
1991 – 1992 Ján Čarnogurský
1992 – 1992 Vladimír Mečiar

THE SLOVAK REPUBLIC

Presidents
1993 – 1998 Michal Kováč
1999 –   Rudolf Schuster

Prime Ministers
1993 – 1994 Vladimír Mečiar
1994 – 1994 Jozef Moravčik
1994 – 1998 Vladimír Mečiar
1998 –   Mikuláš Dzurinda

Bibliography

English Language Sources

BOOKS

Arnott, P., 1973. *The Byzantines and Their World.* New York. St. Martin's Press
Boyle, L., 1989. *A Short Guide to St. Clement's Rome.* Rome. Collegio San Clemente
Bugalová, E., 1993. *Trnava Guide.* Trnava. Town Hall Trnava
Bury, J. B., 1965. *A History of the Eastern Roman Empire.* New York. Russel and Russel
Capek, T., 1906. *The Slovaks of Hungary.* New York. Knickerbocker Press
Cincik, J., 1984. *One Hundred Famous Slovak Men.* Cambridge. Friends of Good Books
Constantine the Philosopher (St. Cyril), 1996. *The Proglas.* Bratislava. Herba
Dekan, J., 1981. *Moravia Magna.* Minneapolis. Control Data Arts Publishers
Donovan, H., (et al.), 1969. *Time Capsule/1968.* New York, Time-Life Books
Durant, W., 1950. *The Story of Civilization, Vol. IV, The Age of Faith.* New York. Simon and Schuster
Durant, W., 1957. *The Story of Civilization, Vol. VI, The Reformation.* New York. Simon and Schuster
Dvornik, F., 1970. *Byzantine Missions Among the Slavs.* New Brunswick. Rutgers University Press
Dvornik, F., 1962. *The Slavs in European History and Civilization.* New Brunswick. Rutgers University Press
Gallio, P., 1998. *The Basilica of Saint Praxedes.* Genova. Edizione d'Arte Marconi
Gimbutas, M., 1971. *The Slavs.* New York. Praeger Publishers
Glaser, K., 1961. *Czecho-Slovakia, A Critical History.* Caldwell. Caxton Printers, Ltd.
Grosvenor, E., 1895. *Constantinople, Volumes I & II.* Boston. Roberts Brothers
Guirand, F., (et al.), 1959. *Larousse Encyclopedia of Mythology.* London. Paul Hamlyn Publishers
Hetherington, P. and Forman, W., 1985. *Byzantium: City of Gold, City of Faith.* London. Orbis
Holčík, Š. and Štefanovičová, T., 1982. *The Castle of Bratislava.* Bratislava. Obzor
Hrušovský, F., 1954. *This is Slovakia.* Scranton. Obrana Press
Hviezdoslav, Országh P., 1950. *Bloody Sonnets.* Scranton. Obrana Press
Ihnat, J., (et al.), 1981. *General Milan Rastislav Štefánik.* New York. Slovak American Cultural Center in New York

BIBLIOGRAPHY

Johnson, L. 1996. *Central Europe.* Oxford University Press. New York

Kirschbaum, J., (et al.), 1978. *Slovak Culture through the Centuries.* Toronto. Slovak World Congress

Kirschbaum, J., 1975. *Slovak Language and Literature.* Winnipeg. University of Manitoba

Kirschbaum, J., (et al.), 1973. *Slovakia in the 19th and 20th Century.* Toronto. Slovak World Congress

Kirschbaum, S., 1995. *A History of Slovakia.* New York. St. Martin's Press

Kirschbaum, S. and Roman, A., eds., 1987. *Reflections on Slovak History.* Toronto. Slovak World Congress

Kona, Mistina M., 1996. *Doctoral Dissertations in Slovakiana in the Western World.* Martin. Matica Slovenská

Kramoris I. 1947. *An Anthology of Slovak Poetry.* Scranton. Obrana Press

Kružliak, I. and Mizenko, F., eds., 1985. *SS. Cyril and Methodius among the Slovaks.* Middletown. Slovak Catholic Federation

Lacko, M., 1969. *Saints Cyril and Methodius.* Rome. Slovak Editions

Lechner, D., ed., 1992. *From Slavonic Liturgy to the Slovak Province.* Bratislava. Univerzitná knižnica

Macartney, C. A., 1965. *Hungary and Her Successors.* London. Oxford University Press

Marko, A. and Martinický, P. 1995. *Slovak-Magyar Relations: History and Present Day in Figures.* Bratislava. Slovak Society for Protection of Democracy and Humanity

McEvedy, C., 1992. *The New Penguin Atlas of Medieval History.* London. Penguin Books

Mikuš, J., 1977. *Slovakia and the Slovaks.* Washington. Three Continents Press

Mináč, V. (et al.), 1995. *Slovaks and Magyars: Slovak-Magyar Relations in Central Europe.* Bratislava: Ministerstvo kultúry Slovenskej republiky

Oddo, G., 1960. *Slovakia and Its People.* New York. Robert Speller and Sons Publishers

Okey, R., 1986. *Eastern Europe 1740 – 1985.* Minneapolis. University of Minnesota Press

Palickar, S., 1954. *Slovakian Culture in the Light of History.* Cambridge. The Hampshire Press

Pearson, R., 1986. *National Minorities in Eastern Europe 1848 – 1945.* London. The MacMillan Press Ltd.

Polcin, S., 1981. *This is the Heritage of Our Fathers.* Cambridge. Friends of Good Books

Portal, R., 1969. *The Slavs.* New York. Harper and Row Publishers

Rekem, J., 1969. *Zobor: The Mount and The Monastery.* Hamilton. Slovak Publishing

Robinson, Spencer H. and Wilson, K., 1961. *Myths and Legends of All Nations.* New York. Bantam Books

Ruggieri V. 1991. *Byzantine Religious Architecture (582 – 867): Its History and Structural Elements.* Rome. Pontificium Institutum Studiorum Orientalium

Scott, S., 1989. *The Collapse of the Moravian Mission of Saints Cyril and Methodius.* Ann Arbor. UMI Dissertation Services

Seton-Watson, R., 1965. *A History of the Czechs and Slovaks.* Hamden. Archon Books

Škultéty, J., 1930. *Sketches from Slovak History.* Middletown. First Catholic Slovak Union

Taylor, E., 1963. *The Fall of the Dynasties.* Garden City. Doubleday and Company

Valent, S., 1992. *Nitra, A Guidebook.* Banská Bystrica. ArtPress

Young, G., 1992. *Constantinople.* New York. Barnes and Noble

Yurchak, P., 1946. *The Slovaks.* Whiting. Obrana Press

Zubek, T., 1956. *The Church of Silence in Slovakia.* Whiting. John J. Lach Publishers

ARTICLES

Hammer, L. „*Za tú našu slovenčinu – The Slovak Language*", The Slovak American Newsletter, July 1993 (Volume 3, Number 2) pp. 8 – 10.
Kirschbaum, S. „*The Czech Question in Slovakia in the Post-War Years*", Slovakia. 35, nos. 64 – 65 (1991 – 1992): 97 – 108
Krostenko, B. „*Slovak and Indo-European*", The Slovak American Newsletter, March 1991 (Volume 1, Number 1) pp. 4 – 6
Mikula, S. „*Relations Between Slovaks and Czechs in the First CSR*", Slovakia. 35, nos. 64 – 65 (1991 – 1992): 78 – 96

Slovak Language Sources

BOOKS

Bagin, A., 1993. *Cyrilometodská tradícia u Slovákov*. Bratislava. Slovak Academic Press
Bagin, A., 1992. *Život Gorazda*. Martin. Matica Slovenská
Bajaník, S., 1993. *Slovensko sa rodilo v Nitre*. Martin. Matica Slovenská
Bárta, V., 1993. *Slovensko/Slovakia*. Martin. Neografia
Baxa, P., and Ferus, V., 1991. *Bratislava mešťana Wocha*. Prievidza. Tlačiareň Patria
Belas, L., (et al.), 1998. *Významné osobnosti Nitry*. Nitra. Nitrianske tlačiarne, a.s.
Bialeková, D., 1981. *Dávne slovanské kováčstvo*. Bratislava. Tatran
Čajak, J., 1914. *Dejiny Slovákov*. Pittsburgh. Tlač Narodných novín
Chalupka, S., 1953. *Mor ho*. Bratislava. Hviezdoslavova knižnica
Čilinská, Z., 1981. *Kov v ranoslovanskom umení*. Bratislava. Tatran
Čulen, K., 1947. *Po Svätoplukovi druhá naša hlava – Život Dr. Jozefa Tisu*. Middletown: Jednota Printery
Ďurica, M., 1995. *Dejiny Slovenska a Slovákov*. Košice. Pressko
Felcán, A., 1932. *Hlohovecko kedysi, dnes a zajtra*. Senica. Tlačiareň Jozefa Löfflera
Feráková, V., (et al.), 1968. *Hlohovec a jeho okolie*. Bratislava. Obzor
Ferko, M., 1993. *Staré povesti slovenské*. Bratislava. Mladé letá
Ferko, M., 1990. *Veľkomoravské záhady*. Bratislava. Tatran
Ferko, M., (et al.). 1994. *Starý národ – mladý štát*. Bratislava. Litera
Fiala, A. and Fialová, H., 1966. *Hrady na Slovensku*. Bratislava. Obzor
Furmánek, V. and Pieta, K. 1985. *Počiatky odievania na Slovensku*. Bratislava. Tatran
Furmánek, V., Ruttkay, A. and Šiška, S., 1991. *Dejiny dávnovekého Slovenska*. Bratislava. Tatran
Hnilica, J., 1988. *Svätí Cyril a Metod*. Rome. Unitas et Pax
Horák, J., 1958. *Slovenské ľudové balady*. Bratislava. Slovenské vydavateľstvo krásnej literatúry
Hrnko, A. and Siváková, D., 1997. *Národná rada Slovenskej republiky*. Bratislava. Atrakt
Huba, P., 1986. *Oravský hrad*. Martin. Osveta
Hudec, D., 1994. *Veľký omyl Veľká Morava*. Martin. Matica slovenská/Neografia
Kleň, M., 1992. *Súbežnice života oravského človeka*. Vrútky. NADAS-AFGH, s.r.o.

Kollár, J., 1924. *Slávy dcéra z roku 1824*. Turčiansky Svätý Martin. Matica Slovenská
Konus, J., 1969. *Slovak-English Phraseological Dictionary*. Passaic. Slovak Catholic Sokol
Krajčovič, R., ed., 1985. *Veľká Morava v tisícročí*. Bratislava. Tatran
Konštantín Filozof (Sv. Cyril). 1996. *Proglas*. Bratislava. Herba
Kráľ, J., 1949. *Výlomky z Jánošíka*. Bratislava. Tatran
Kučera, M., 1985. *Metod – učiteľ Slovienov*. Martin. Matica Slovenská
Lacko, M., 1993. *Svätý Cyril a Metod*. Rome. Slovenský ústav
Lajoš, J. (et al.), 1964. *Nitra: Slovom i obrazom*. Nitra. Okresné vlastivedné múzeum. Polygrafické závody
Langer, J. (et al.), 1993. *Cesty po minulosti Oravy*. Dolný Kubín. Peter Huba
Lechner, D., ed., 1992. *Od slovienskej liturgie ku slovenskej provincii*. Bratislava. Univerzitná knižnica
Marsina, R., 1997. *Legendy stredovekého Slovenska*. Nitra. Vydavateľstvo Rak
Novák, J., 1967. *Slovenské mestské a obecné erby*. Bratislava. Slovenská archívna správa
Okál, J., 1975. *Kronika Slovákov*. Cambridge. Friends of Good Books
Pieta, K. and Jakab, J., 1993. *Nitra. Príspevky k najstarším dejinám mesta*. Nitra. Archeologický ústav SAV
Plachá, V. (et al.), 1990. *Slovanský Devín*. Bratislava. Obzor
Ratkoš, P. 1988. *Slovensko v dobe Veľkomoravskej*. Košice. Východoslovenské vydavateľstvo
Ratkoš, P., ed. 1990. *Veľkomoravské legendy a povesti*. Bratislava. Tatran
Ruttkay, A., 1978. *Umenie kované v zbraniach*. Bratislava. Pallas
Ruttkay, A. and Čelko, E., 1984. *Kostolec – archeologická rezervácia – Moravany nad Váhom – Ducové pri Piešťanoch*. Piešťany. Západoslovenské tlačiarne
Ruttkay, A. and Veliká, D., 1993. *Nitra*. Bratislava. Davel
Sládkovič, A., 1965. *Marína*. Bratislava. Slovenské vydavateľstvo krásnej literatúry
Štefanovičová, T., 1989. *Osudy starých Slovanov*. Martin. Osveta
Tassy, J. (et al.), 1989. *Hlohovec*. Bratislava. Obzor
Tibenský, J. (et al.), 1978. *Slovensko. Dejiny*. Bratislava. Obzor
Varsik, M., 1990. *M. R. Štefánik*. Bratislava. Biofond OVD Bratislava
Veteška, T., 1987. *Veľkoslovenská ríša*. Hamilton. Zahraničná Matica Slovenská
Vladár, J. 1983. *Dávne kultúry a Slovensko*. Bratislava. Tatran
Vragaš, Š. and Bagin, A., 1994. *Život Konštantína Cyrila a život Metoda*. Martin. Matica Slovenská
Zrubec, L., 1991. *Osobnosti našej minulosti*. Bratislava. Slovenské pedagogické nakladateľstvo
Zrubec, L., 1994. *Prvý známy bol Pribina*. Bratislava. Slovenské pedagogické nakladateľstvo

PAMPHLETS

Obecný úrad Habovka, Júl, 1993. *Habovka 1593 – 1993, pri príležitosti 400. výročia prvej písomnej zmienky o obci*

Glossary

Alkopion: *Greek* – A religious object, such as a cross or medallion, decorated with Christian imagery, often encasing a relic and worn on a chain around the neck.

Acquincum: *Latin* – Roman name for what is today Budapest, Hungary.

Ausgleich: *German* – Union of the Austrian Empire and the multinational kingdom of Hungary in 1867 that created the dual monarchy of the Austro-Hungarian empire.

Ban: *Persian* – (lit. 'lord' or 'master') Title used for a governor of a banat (province) in the multinational kingdom of Hungary.

Basileus: *Greek* – (lit. 'king') Principal title of the Byzantine Emperor.

Basilica Liberiana: *Latin* – Original Roman name for the Basilica of St. Mary Major; from the name of Pope Liberius.

Basilica of the Phatne: *Greek* – The Basilica of the Manager; Greek name for the Basilica of St. Mary Major in Rome, Italy.

bes: *Slovak* – A demon or evil spirit.

bielobožstvá: *Slovak* – In Slovak mythology, the Forces or Deities of Light.

bielokňaz: *Slovak* – Pagan Slovak priest, serving the Forces of Light.

Biharia: *Latin* – Medieval principality that today forms the northeastern part of Hungary and the northwestern part of Rumania.

Blatnohrad: *Slovak* – The name of an Old Slovak settlement in what is now present day Hungary; now known as Zalavár.

Bolo i bude: *Slovak* – It Was and Will Be; poem by Samoslav Chalupka in Slovak Literature.

Brezalauspurch: *Frankish* – The name of the Franks for Bratslav's or Preslav's Castle, i.e., Bratislava Castle.

Brigetium: *Latin* – Roman name for the Slovak municipality of Komárno.

bryndza: *Rumanian* – A type of Slovakian sheep's cheese.

Carnuntum: *Latin* – Roman name for what is now Petronell, Austria.

chartophylax: *Greek* – An administrative post in imperial Byzantium which combined the duties of patriarchal secretary and librarian.

čarodejník: *Slovak* – Magician, enchanter.

červení mnísi: *Slovak* – (lit. 'the Red Monks') The Slovak term for the Knights Templar.

čiernobožstvá: *Slovak* – In Slovak mythology, the Dark Forces or Dieties.

čiernokňažníctvo: *Slovak* – Pagan Slovak priesthood serving the Dark Forces.

GLOSSARY

čiernokňažník: *Slovak* – Pagan Slovak sorcerer, or priests, serving the Dar1k Forces.
Cuius regio eius religio: *Latin* – (lit. 'As the king, so the religion') – The ruler's religion is the realm's religion.

ďas: *Slovak* – In Slovak mythology, a pagan devil god or spirit.

Ekloge: *Greek* – Byzantine Codex of Civil Law.

Gerulata: *Latin* – Roman name for the Slovak municipality of Rusovce (now a part of the city of Bratislava).
Grammatica Slavica: *Latin* – Anton Bernolák's codification of the Slovak language, published in 1790.

Hájnikova žena: *Slovak* – The Forester's Wife; lyrical epic by Pavol Országh Hviezdoslav, in Slovak Literature.
Hlaholika: *Slovak* – The Glagolitic alphabet composed by Constantine-Cyril.

incunabula: *Latin* – Book or manuscript produced before the year 1501 A.D.
Industriae Tuae: *Latin* – (lit. 'Concerning Your Endeavors') Papal Bull, which established Nitra as the first Slovak bishopric, recognized Old Slavonic, the forerunner of modern Slovak, as a liturgical language alongside Latin, Greek and Hebrew and acknowledged the kingship of Svätopluk.
intaglio: *Italian* – A form of printing, such as a gravure.
Iskoni bie Slovo: *Old Slavonic* – In the beginning was the word.
Istropolis: *Greek* – Greek name for Slovakia's capital city of Bratislava.

khagan: *Oriental* – Title of an Avar ruler.

knieža: *Slovak* – Prince.
Koleda: *Slovak* – Old Slovak pagan term for the winter solstice; modern Slovak a Christmas carol.
Krvavé sonety: *Slovak* – Bloody Sonnets; poetry by Pavol Országh Hviezdoslav, in Slovak Literature.

lebensraum: *German* – Living space or room to grow; a phrase used to promote Nazi Germany's desire for expansion.
lesná panna: *Slovak* – In Slovak mythology, a forest maiden.
Letnice: *Slovak* – In pagan times, a Slovak term for the summer solstice; in modern Slovak it refers to the Christian feast of Pentecost.
Limes Romanus: *Latin* – Roman Frontier; outlying borders of the Roman Empire.
lingua franca: *Latin* – (lit. 'the Frankish Language') A language used universally as a common language.
Logos: *Greek* – The Word.
loktibrada: *Slovak* – In Slovak mythology, a troll.

Maďarsko: *Slovak* – Slovak name for present day Hungary.
Magyarország: *Magyar-Hungarian* – Magyar name for present day Hungary.
Maria Santissima Liberatrice: *Italian* – (lit. 'Our Lady of Deliverance') A title of the Virgin Mary.
Matica Slovenská: *Slovak* – The name of Slovakia's premier, national, cultural repository and historical archive.
Megalo Ecclesia: *Greek* – (lit. 'the Great Church').
megalomartyr: *Greek* – (lit. 'the great martyr').
mohyla: *Slovak* – An earthen work burial mound or cairn.
Mor ho: *Slovak* – (lit. 'Crush him') An epic poem by Samoslav Chalupka in Slovak Literature.
Moravské Slovácko: *Slovak* – The region of Moravian Slovakia.

Na počiatku bolo Slovo a Slovo bolo u Boha a Boh bol Slovo: *Slovak* – In the beginning was the Word, and the Word was with God, and the Word was God.
náčelník: *Slovak* – Chieftain.

Ostrihom: *Slovak* – Slovakian name for what is today the city of Esztergom in the Republic of Hungary. It is situated across the Danube River from the Slovak town of Štúrovo. Originally it was the Roman town of Strigonium and at one point served as the capital of the multi-national kingdom of Hungary. From 1543 to 1595 and again from 1604 to 1683 it was under Turkish rule. It is a Roman Catholic archiepiscopal see and the seat of a cardinal-primate.

Panna Mária Sedembolestná: *Slovak* – (lit. 'Our Lady of the Seven Sorrows') A title of the Virgin Mary; also the title under which she is honored as the national Patroness of Slovakia.
Parom ho trafil: *Slovak* – (lit. 'Parom has struck him down').
Phatne: *Greek* – A crib or manger.
piadimužík: *Slovak* – A dwarf.
pikulík: *Slovak* – In Slovak mythology, a gnome.
popolnica: *Slovak* – A pagan Slovak clay burial urn.
Posonium: *Latin* – Roman name for Slovakia's capital city of Bratislava.
Pozsony: *Magyar-Hungarian* – Magyar name for Slovakia's capital city of Bratislava; it is a corruption of Posonium, the old Roman name for Bratislava.
Praesepe: *Latin* – A crib or manger.
Pressalauspurch: *Frankish* – The Old Frankish name for Bratslav's or Preslav's Castle, i.e, Bratislava Castle.
Pressburg: *German* – The Austrian name for Slovakia's capital city of Bratislava, from the old Frankish, Brezalauspurch/Pressalauspurch.

Proglas: *Old Slavonic* – A religious treatise written by St. Constantine-Cyril.
Pyxidium: *Latin, from Greek* – A circular box, often used as a reliquary or to hold valuables.

Rusadlá: *Slovak* – In pagan times, a Slovak term for the summer solstice; in modern Slovak it refers to the Christian feast of Pentecost.
rusalka: *Slovak* – In Slovak mythology, a treacherous type of water nymph.

salaš: *Slovak* – A Slovakian sheep farm.
Sancta Maria ad Nives: *Latin* – (lit. 'Our Lady of the Snows') An old Roman name for the Basilica Liberiana, now known as St. Mary Major.
Sancta Maria ad Praesepe: *Latin* – (lit. 'Our Lady of the Manger') Another name for the Basilica of St. Mary Major in Rome, Italy.
Singidunum: *Latin* – Roman name for the city of Belgrade in Serbia.

Slováci: *Slovak* – The plural of the word Slovak, i.e., Slovaks.
Slověne: *Old Slavonic* – An archaic form for the word Slovak.
Slovenské učené tovaryšstvo: *Slovak* – The Slovak Learned Society founded in 1792 to promote and foster Slovak literature and learning.
Slovensko: *Slovak* – The Slovakian name for the country of Slovakia.
slovienčina: *Slovak* – The Old Slavonic/Old Slovak language.
Slovieni: *Slovak* – Original name of the Slovaks for themselves.
slovienska: *Slovak* – Feminine descriptive adjective, meaning Old Slavonic or Old Slovak.
sloviensky: *Slovak* – Masculine descriptive adjective; see above
slovo: *Slovak* – Word, or the word.
Solúň: *Slovak* – Slovak name for the Greek city

of Thessalonika, the birthplace of Constantine-Cyril and Methodius.

Smrť Jánošíkova: *Slovak* – (lit. 'The Death of Jánošík'); An epic poem, in Slovak Literature, by the poet, Ján Botto (1829 – 1881).

Smútok: *Slovak* – (lit. 'Sorrow') A poem by Samoslav Chalupka in Slovak Literature

Staré mesto: *Slovak* – (lit. 'Old Town') The medieval old town area of a Slovak city versus its modern counterpart.

Stoličný Belehrad: *Slovak* – Slovakian name for what is todaay the city of Székesfehérvár in the Republic of Hungary. Originally it was the Roman town of Alba Regia. It was the capital of the multi-ethnic kingdom of Hungary until the fourteenth century and the coronation site of its kings from 1027 until 1527. From 1543 to 1686 it was under the Turks. In 1563 the City of Bratislava became the new coronation site of the kingdom and remained so until 1830.

Te Deum: *Latin* – (lit. 'To You, O God') Solemn Roman Catholic religious hymn sung in praise and thanksgiving to glorify God.

Theotokos: *Greek* – (lit. 'The Godbearer' or 'the Mother of God') A title of the Virgin Mary.

Tót nem ember: *Magyar-Hungarian* – (lit. 'A Slovak is not a human being') A derogatory pronouncement of Magyar-Hungarian extremists in use in the late nineteenth, early twentieth centuriues.

Triglav/Trihlav: *Slovak* – The Three-Headed one; pagan Slovak divinity.

Turíce: *Slovak* – In pagan times, a Slovak term for the summer solstice; in modern Slovak it refers to the Christian feast of Pentecost.

Uhorsko: *Slovak* – Slovakian name for the multi-national kingdom of Hungary, of which Slovakia formed the upper or northern part.

Uhri/Ugri: *Slovak* – Name of an Asiatic group akin to the Samoyeds of Northeastern Siberia; the ancestors of the Magyars.

vedomkyňa (pl. vedomkyne): *Slovak* – Seeress or prophetess.

Veľká Morava: *Slovak* – Great Moravia, name of the ninth century Slovakian Empire.

veštica: *Slovak* – fortune-teller.

víla: *Slovak* – In Slovak mythology, a water nymph.

Vindobona: *Latin* – Roman name for what is now Vienna, Austria.

vlkodlak: *Slovak* – In Slovak mythology, a were-wolf.

vodník: *Slovak* – In Slovak mythology a water spirit.

vojvoda: *Slovak* – Duke.

žertva: *Slovak* – Pagan Slovak sacrificial offerings in the form of grains, plants or animals.

žinčica: *Slovak* – The boiled sweet whey from bryndza cheese.

Život Metoda: *Slovak* – The Life of Methodius, written in Old Slavonic and attributed to Methodius' protegé, the Slovak saint, Gorazd.

žrec: *Slovak* – A priest belonging to the old Slovak pagan priestly sacrificial caste.

Picture Credits

The sources for the illustrations that appear in this work are as follows. Credits from top to bottom are separated by hyphens.

Inside front cover: Engraving of Bratislava from 1684, Matica slovenská Archives, Martin. **2:** Mikuláš Klimčák, Bratislava. **5:** Klimek Ward Coat-of-Arms, Slovak College of Arms, Bratislava. **15:** Map, Mapa Slovakia, Bratislava and Nitra Information System Office, Nitra. **19 – 20:** Vzlet Publications, Čadca. **21 – 22:** Karol Felix, Nitra. **23:** Matica slovenská Archives, Martin. **24:** Nitra Information System Office, Nitra – Matica slovenská Archives, Martin. **25:** Matica slovenská Archives, Martin. **27:** Vzlet Publications, Čadca. **28:** JUDr. Štefan Valent, Nitra; photograph by Marta Novotná, Nitra – Nitra Information System Office, Nitra. **29:** Nitra Information System Office, Nitra. **30 – 31:** Greek National Tourist Organization, New York. **32 – 34:** Art Resource, New York. **35:** Mikuláš Klimčák, Bratislava. **36:** Mikuláš Klimčák, Bratislava – Copyright Calmann & King Ltd, London, reproduced with permission. From Thomas F. Mathews, *Byzantium: From Antiquity to the Renaissance*, 1998. **37:** Matica slovenská Archives, Martin. **38:** Mikuláš Klimčák, Bratislava – Vladimír Čierny, Remium Artistic Productions, Pezinok. **39:** Msgr. František Novajovský, Pontifical Slovak College of Saint Cyril and Saint Methodius, Rome. **40:** B. N. Marconi Arte Grafiche, Genoa, Italy – Andrea Urlandová, Bratislava. **41:** Andrea Urlandová, Bratislava. **42:** B. N. Marconi Arte Grafiche, Genoa, Italy. **43:** Irish Dominican Fathers, Rome. **44:** B. N. Marconi Arte Grafiche, Genoa – College of Santa Maria Maggiore, Rome. **45:** College of Santa Maria Maggiore, Rome. **46:** Andrea Urlandová, Bratislava – Irish Dominican Fathers, Rome. **47:** Irish Dominican Fathers, Rome. **48:** Irish Dominican Fathers, Rome. **50:** Irish Dominican Fathers, Rome. **51:** Irish Dominican Fathers, Rome – Paul Victor Gallo, Naperville, Illinois. **52:** Nitra Information System Office, Nitra – Vlastivedné múzeum and Archives, Hlohovec. **53:** Matica slovenská Archives, Martin – Nitra Information System Office, Nitra. **54:** JUDr. Štefan Valent; photograph by Marta

PICTURE CREDITS

Novotná, Nitra – Marta Novotná, Nitra – City of Hlohovec. **57:** Matica slovenská Archives, Martin. **58:** Matica slovenská Archives, Martin. **59:** Matica slovenská Archives, Martin. **60 – 63:** Matica slovenská Archives, Martin. **64:** Vzlet Publications, Čadca – Matica slovenská Archives, Martin. **66:** Matica slovenská Archives, Martin. **67 – 69:** Vlastivedné múzeum and Archives, Hlohovec. **70:** Vlastivedné múzeum and Archives, Hlohovec – City of Hlohovec. **72:** Orava Museum, Dolný Kubin – Orava Art Gallery, Dolný Kubin. **73 – 74:** Lydia Vojtaššáková, Habovka. **75:** Lydia Vojtaššáková, Habovka – Vladimír Žuffa, Zuberec. **76:** Lydia Vojtaššáková, Habovka – Matica Slovenská Archives, Martin. **77:** Vladimír Žuffa, Zuberec. **78:** Múzeum Martina Benka, Martin. **79:** Mikuláš Klimčák, Bratislava – Vzlet Publications, Čadca. **80:** Vzlet Publications, Čadca. **83 – 84:** Matica slovenská Archives, Martin. **85:** Matica slovenská Archives, Martin – Vzlet Publications, Čadca. **86:** Vlastivedné múzeum and Archives, Hlohovec. **87:** Matica slovenská Archives, Martin. **95:** Matica Slovenská Archives, Martin, from Publication: R. Holec: Tragédia v Černovej a slovenská spoločnosť. **96:** Matica slovenská Archives, Martin. **97 – 98:** Vzlet Publications, Čadca. **99:** Dagmar Veliká, Bratislava – Seminary of Sts. Cyril and Methodius, Bratislava. **100:** Mikuláš Klimčák, Bratislava. **101:** Matica slovenská Archives, Martin. **103 – 104:** Matica slovenská Archives, Martin. **Inside back cover:** Engraving of Košice from 1700, Matica slovenská Archives, Martin.

Index

About the Kingdom and the Kings of the Slovaks, 71
About the Oldest Site of Great Moravia, 71
Academia Istropolitana, 61
Acquincum, 47
Adalram,. Archbishop of Salzburg, 28
Albert of Habsburg, King, 61
Albgis, 37
Alexander the Great, 30
Alexander VI, Pope, 41
Alexius I Comnenus, Byzantine Emperor, 57
All Saints, Franciscan Monastery of, Hlohovec, 70
Allied Powers, 102
Amber Route, 23, 72
American Revolution, 82
Ammianus Marcellinus, 18
Andrássy, Julius, Hungarian Prime Minister, 91
Andrew III, King, 59
Angelár, 43
Apponyi, Albert, 93
Apponyi Law, 93
Asia, 17, 27
Arpád family, 56, 59
Augsburg, 55
Ausgleich of 1867, 90
Austria-Hungary, 83, 90, 100
Austrian empire, 66, 84, 86
Austrian government, 89
Austrians, 88
Avars, 27
Axis Powers, 102

Bajan, Avar khagan, 27
Balaton, Lake, 31
Banská Bystrica, 87, 90
Banská Štiavnica, 69
Basil I, Byzantine Emperor, 43
Basilica Liberiana, Rome, 39
Basilicas:
  Liberiana, Rome, 39
  Phatne, Rome, 39
  St. Clement, Rome, 41, 43, 46 – 48, 50 – 51
  St. George the Great Martyr, Thessalonika, 30
  St. John Lateran, Rome, 41
  St. Mary Major, Rome, 39, 44 – 46
  St. Paul Outside the Walls, Rome, 41
  St. Peter, Rome, 41
  St. Praxedes, Rome, 40, 42, 44
  Sancta Maria ad Nives, Rome, 39
  Sancta Maria ad Praesepe, Rome, 39
Batu Khan, 59
Belgrade, 47
Belo IV, King, 59
Benedictine Monks, 29
Beneš, Edvard, 96, 98, 102
Bernolák, Anton, 69, 71, 80 – 82
besovia, 19
Bethlehem, Manger of, 39
Bethlen, Gábor, 67
Bielboh, 18
bielobožstvá, 19
bielokňazi, 19
Biharia, 57
Bíňa, 25
Blatnohrad, 25, 31
Bocskay, Štefan, 67
Bohemia, 95 – 96, 100
Bolo i bude, 82

Botto, Ján, 69
Brandýs, 61
Bratislava, 18, 23, 27, 43, 47, 59, 63, 67, 96, 99 – 100, 103 – 104
Bratislava, Battle of, 49
Bratislava Castle, 25, 47, 49, 55
Bratislav, Prince, 45, 47, 54 – 55
Brezalauspurch, 47
Brezová, 88
Brigetium, 47
Budapest, 47, 63, 82, 86, 88 – 91, 93
Bujak, 66
Bulgar alliance, 33
Bytča, Castle of, 58
Byzantine Codex of Civil Law, 35
Byzantium, 33, 63

Camaldolese Monks, 29
Capek, Thomas, 91
Carloman, 37, 43, 45
Carnuntum, 47
Carpathian Mountains, 27
Cassander, 30
Cassius Dio, 17
Castles:
  Bratislava, 25, 47, 49, 55
  Bytča, 58
  Devín, 23 – 24, 27, 31, 37, 43, 45, 47, 53
  Hlohovec, 66 – 67
  Nitra, 24, 53
  Orava, 72 – 73
  Spiš, 58
  Strečno, 62
  Topoľčany, 61
  Trenčín, 59 – 60
  Vosgate, 27

121

INDEX

Vratislav, 47
Catholic Counter-Reformation, 63, 65, 57
Cathedrals:
 Hagia Sophia/(Megalo Ecclesia, Constantinople, 32 – 34, 36
 Holy Savior, Bratislava, 99
 St. Elizabeth, Košice, 62
 St. Emeram, Nitra, 29, 54
 St. Martin, Bratislava, 99, 104
Celts, 17, 21, 23, 25
Chalupka, Samoslav, 82
Chapels:
 St. Cyril and St. Methodius, Chapels of, Rome, 39, 43
 St. Mary Magdalene, Habovka, 74
 St. Zeno, Rome, 42, 44
Charlemagne, 27
Charles V, Duke of Lorraine, 63
Charles Robert of Anjou, King, 60, 63
chartophylax, 37
Churches:
 Our Lady of the Seven Sorrows, Habovka, 74
 St. Martin, Nitra, 29
 St. Michael the Archangel, Hlohovec, 23, 68 – 69
Cieszyn, 101
Class Wars, 67
Claudius Ptolemy, 18
Clement I, St., Pope, 46, 48
Clement XI, Pope, 47
Coelian Hill, 41
Communism, 102 – 103
Conchessa, mother of St. Patrick, 99
Constantine the Great, Roman Emperor, 33
Constantine VII Porphyrogenitus, Byzantine Emperor, 31
Constantine-Cyril, St., 26, 30, 33, 35 – 41, 43, 45 – 46, 48, 69, 90
Constantinople, 33, 36, 52, 57, 61, 66, 90
Cracovia, 47
Croatia, 86
Croatian parliament, 86
Croatians, 81, 84, 86, 98
Crusades, 57
Cyril, St., *see Constantine-Cyril*
Cyrillic alphabet, 35
Cyrilo-Methodiada, 82
Czech tribes, 45, 47

Czechs, 98, 100 – 102
Czechia, 102
Czech Revolutionary National Committee, 96
Czecho-Slovak, 95
Czecho-Slovak Legions, 96
Czecho-Slovakia, 95 – 96, 100, 102 – 104
Czechoslovak, 98
Czechoslovak Socialist Republic, 103
Czechoslovakia, 102
Czechoslovakism, 98
čarodejníci, 19
Černová, 94
Černová, Massacre of, 94 – 95
Červení mníši, 57
Český Těšín, 101
Čierne Kľačany, 25, 52
Čiernoboh, 18, 21
čiernobožstvá, 19
čiernokňažníci, 19
čiernokňažníctvo, 19

Dagobert, King of the Franks, 27
Danube river, 17, 27, 31, 37, 66, 100
Danubian basin, 27
ďasovia, 19
Daxner, Štefan Marko, 82, 89
Dažboh, 18
Dcéra Slávy, 21 – 22
Detvan, 82
Devín Castle, 23 – 24, 27, 31, 37, 43, 45, 47, 53
Devínska Nová Ves, 21
Devojna, 47
Divinka-Žilina, 25
Dual Monarchy, 90
Dubček, Alexander, 82, 103
Ducové, 25

Early Slav, 17
Eastern Mark, 31, 35
Ečer, Bohumil, 102
Ekloge, 35
Elentheroepolis, 23
Elizabeth, Queen, wife of Albert of Habsburg, 61
Ellwangen, 37
Engelschalk, 45
England, 102
English language, 100
Esquilline Hill, 39

Europe, 17, 65 – 67, 95

Far East, 96
Felvidék, 91
Ferdinand I (V), Habsburg Emperor, 84
Ferdinand the Catholic, King of Spain, 41
Fiľakovo, 66
Forchheim, Treaty of, 45
France, 96, 102
Francis Joseph I, Habsburg Emperor, 89 – 90
Francisci-Rimavský, Jan, 82, 89
Frankish chroniclers, 31, 67
Frankish missionaries, 33
Franks, 33, 38, 43, 45, 47, 55
French Revolution, 82
Friars Minor (Franciscans), 70
Fulda, Annals of, 67

Galerius, Arch of, Thessalonika, 31
Galerius, Roman Emperor, 31
Genghis Khan, 59
Germans, 18, 21, 56, 100,
Germany, 58, 81, 97
Gerulata, 47
Gejza I, King, 57
Glagolitic alphabet, 35, 52
Godbearer/Theotokos, 33 – 34, 41
Gorazd, St., 31, 38, 43
Gorbachev, Mikhail, 104
Goths, 17
Grammatica Slavica, 71
Great Moravia, 23 – 25, 27, 37, 55, 59
Greek alphabet, 35
Greek language, 41, 45
Greek rite, Monks of the, 35, 40
Greeks, 21
Gregory VII, Pope, 57
Grünwald, Béla, 91 – 92

Habovka, 67, 73 – 74, 76
Habsburgs, 65, 67, 69, 81, 84
Hadrian II, Pope, 39, 43, 45 – 46, 48
Hagia Sophia, Cathedral of, Constantinople, 32 – 34, 36
Hájnikova žena, 82
Hebrew language, 41, 45
Henry III, German Emperor, 57
Henry IV, German Emperor, 57
Hermanaric, Bishop of Passau, 39
Herodotus, 17

INDEX

Hitler, Adolph, 102
Hlaholika alphabet, 35, 52
Hlinka, Andrej Msgr., 82, 93 – 95, 97
Hlohovec, 21, 23, 25, 52, 66 – 70, 86
Hlohovec, Castle of, 66 – 67
Holy Roman Empire, 67
Holy Savior, Cathedral Church of the, Bratislava, 99
Hollý, Ján, 81
Holuby, Karol, 86, 88
Hradčany, 102
Hradec-Prievidza, 25
Hron river, 27
Hungaria, 49
Hungarian Diet, 84, 86, 89 – 90, 93 – 94
Hungarians, 47, 98, 100
Hungary, 25, 49, 56, 57, 60, 66, 81, 84, 89 – 90
Hunyady, John, 61
Hurban, Jozef Miloslav, 82, 86, 88
Hussite wars, 61
Hviezdoslav, Pavol Országh, 82, 87

Ignatius the Younger, Patriarch of Constantinople, 36
India, 17
Indo-European, 17, 56
Industriae Tuae, papal bull, 45
Ireland, 99
Irene, Byzantine Empress, 34
Irish, 98
Isabella, Queen of Spain, 41
Israelis, 98
Istebné-Hrádok, 25
Istropolis, 47
Italy, 96
Ivanka pri Dunaji, 96

Jahelka, Pavel, 23
Jánošík, Juraj, 69, 78 – 79
Jelačič, Josip, Gen., 84, 86
Jewish deportations, 102
Jiskra, Ján, 61
John II Comnenus, Byzantine Emperor, 34
John, St., Gospel of, 26
John VIII, Pope, 45
Jordanes, 18
Justinian I the Great, 32 – 33, 48

Kara Mustafa, Turkish Grand Vizier, 67

Kliment, 43
knieža, 21
Knights Templar, 57
Koceľ, 28, 31
Kollár, Ján, 82 – 83
koleda, 21
Komárno, 47
Korec, Ján Chryzostom, Cardinal-Bishop of Nitra, 35
Košariská, 95
Košice, 18, 60, 62
Kossuth, Lajos, 84, 88
Kossuth gallows, 88
Kráľ, Janko, 82
Krvavé sonety/Bloody Sonnets, 82
Kukučín, Martin, 82

Lada, 19
Ladislav I, King, 34
Ladislav the Posthumous, King, 61
Lateran Palace, 41
Laterani, 41
Latin language, 37, 41, 45, 81, 100
Latin rite, 43
Laugaricio, 27, 59
lebensraum, 102
Lechfeld, 55
lesná panna, 19
Letnice, 21
Levice, 66
Liberius, Pope, 39, 44
"Liberty trees", 88
Life of Methodius, 31
Limes Romanus, 17
Liptov, 21, 57, 94
Liptovský Svätý Mikuláš, 69
Lithuanian forces, 67
loktibrady, 19
Louis the German, King, 31, 33, 37, 43, 45
Louis IX, King of France, 57
Lusatian Serbs, 45
Luther, Martin, 63

Macartney, C.A., 98
Magyar absolutism, 89, 93
Magyarization, 81 – 82, 89, 91, 93
Magyars, 47, 55 – 57, 59, 81, 86, 88 – 89, 92
Majcichov, 25
Marína, 82
Martin, St., Bishop of Tours, 99

Masaryk, Tomáš Garrigue, 96, 101
Matthias Corvinus, King, 61, 64
Matica Slovenská, 52, 90 – 91
Matúš Čak Trenčiansky, 59 – 60, 63 – 64
Mečiar, Vladimír, Prime Minister, 104
Memorandum Slovenského národa/ Memorandum of the Slovak Nation, 82, 89 – 90
Methodius, St., 30, 33, 35, 37 – 41, 43, 45 – 46, 48, 52 – 53, 69, 90
Michael I Rhangabe, Byzantine Emperor, 36
Michael III, Byzantine Emperor, 31, 33, 35, 45, 52
Michael VIII Palaeologus, Byzantine Emperor, 57
Migration of the Nations, 17
Mikulčice, 41
Modra, 84
Mohács, Battle of, 61, 63, 66
Mohammed II, Turkish Sultan, 61
Mohammed IV, Turkish Sultan, 66 – 67
Mohi, Battle of, 59
mohyla, 21
Mojmír I, 29
Mojmír II, Prince 45, 47, 54
Monasteries:
   All Saints, Hlohovec, 70
   St. Hippolytus, Nitra, 29
   St. Praxedes, Rome, 39 – 40
Mor ho, 82
Morava river, 17, 23, 27, 31, 37
Moravia, 88, 96, 100, 102
Moravian Slovakia, 27, 29, 31
Moravians, 31, 45, 83
Morena, 18 – 19, 21
Moscow, 103 – 104
Mount St. Martin, 29
Mount Zobor, 29
Moyses, Štefan, Bishop of Banská Bystrica, 82, 87, 90
Munich Pact, 102
Myjava, 88

náčelník, 21
Napoleonic wars, 83
National Assemblage of 1861, 85, 89
Naum, 43
Nicholas I, Pope, 33, 39,
Nicholas I, Russian Tsar, 89

INDEX

Nitra, 1, 23, 24, 28 – 29, 33, 35, 37, 43, 45, 52, 54, 95
Nitra, Castle of, 24, 53
Nitra river, 27
Nové Zámky, 66
Novohrad, 21, 66

Ogadai Khan, 59
Old Hungarians, 43
Old Slavonic, 26, 35, 45,
Old Slovak, 17, 26, 35, 43
Old Slovaks, 17, 25 – 26, 41
Olomouc, 89
Orava, 67, 69, 72 – 75, 101
Orava, Castle of, 73 – 74
Oravice, 73
Ostrá Skala, 25
Ostrihom, 57, 59
Otto I, German King, 55
Otto of Bavaria (Wittelsbach), King, 60
Our Lady of Deliverance, mosaic of, Rome, 44
Our Lady of the Seven Sorrows, Church of, Habovka, 74
Ourban, Hungarian engineer, 61

Palestinians, 98
Pan-Slav Congress, 86
Pan-Slavic Movement, 83 – 84
Pannonia, 31, 59,
Papánek, Juraj, 71
Parom, 18, 20
Párvy, Alexander, Bishop of Spiš, 94
Pascal I, Pope, 42
Paškievič, Prince Ivan Feodorovič, Russian General, 89
Patrick, St., 99
Paul, St., 30, 40
Pest, 59
Petronell, 47
Phatne, Basilica of the, 39
Philip IV, King of France, 57
Photius I, Patriarch of Constantinople, 34
piadimužíci, 19
pikulíci, 19
Piroška, Princess of Uhorsko, 34
Pittsburgh Agreement, 101
Pliny the Elder, 18
Pobedim, 25
Poland, 67,101
Polish, 83, 98

Pontifical Slovak College of Sts. Cyril and Methodius / Cyrilo-Methodeum, Rome, 39, 51
popolnica, 21
Posonium, 47
Pozsony, 47
Praboh, 18
Prague, 86, 96, 98, 101 – 103
Praxedes, St., 40
Predslav, 45
Preslav, 45
Pressalauspurch, 47
Pressburg, 47
Pribina, Prince, 24, 28 – 29, 31, 43
Procopius, 18
Proglas, The, 350
Protestant Reformation, 63, 65, 67
proto-Slav, 17
proto-Slovak, 17
proto-Slovaks, 17
Prussia, 86
Pudens, Roman Senator, 40

Radhosť, 18
Rákoci, František, 67
Rákoci I, Juraj, 67
Rákoci II, Juraj, 67
Rastislav, Prince, 23, 31, 33, 35, 37, 52
Rastislav, 82
Rathbod, 31
Red Monks, 57
Regensburg, 47
Revolution of 1848, 84, 86, 89
Roháče, 73, 77
Roman Curia, 43, 94
Romanians, 81
Romans, 23, 25, 27, 59
Rome, 33, 39
Rozhanovce, 60, 63
Rusadlá, 21
rusalka, 19
Rusins, 81, 83
Rusovce, 45
Russia, 89
Russians, 83, 89
Ruthenia, 96, 100

Sady, 41
St. Clement, Basilica of, Rome, 41, 43, 46 – 48, 50 – 51
St. Cyril and St. Methodius, chapels of, Rome, 39, 43

St. Elizabeth, Cathedral of, Košice, 62
St. Emeram, Cathedral of, Nitra, 29, 54
St. George the Great Martyr, Basilica of, Thessalonika, 30
St. Hippolytus, Monastery of, Nitra, 29
St. John Lateran, Basilica of, Rome, 41
St, Martin, Co-Cathedral of, Bratislava, 99, 104
St. Martin, Church of, Nitra, 29
St. Mary Major, Basilica of, Rome, 39, 44 – 46
St. Mary Magdalene, Chapel of, Habovka, 74
St. Michael the Archangel, Church of, Hlohovec, 23, 68 – 69
St. Paul Outside the Walls, Basilica of, Rome, 41
St. Peter, Basilica of, Rome, 41
St. Praxedes, Basilica of, Rome, 35, 37, 39
St. Praxedes, Monastery of, Rome, 39 – 40
St. Zeno, Chapel of, Rome, 42, 44
Samo, 27
Samo's Empire, 27
Samoyeds, 49
Sancta Maria ad Nives, Basilica of, Rome, 39
Sancta Maria ad Praesepe, Basilica of, Rome, 39
Sapieha, Casimir, 67
Sava, 43
Serbia, 86
Serbs, 86
Servians, 91
Seton-Watson, R.W., 92
Siberia, 96
Siladice, 25
Silesians, 45
Singidunum, 47
Skalica, 21, 25
Sklenár, Juraj, 71
Skyčák, František, 93
Sládkovič, Andrej, 82
Slaná River, Battle of the, 59
Slanica, 69
Slav, 82
Slavs, 17, 18
Slávy dcéra, 82
Slavonic Liturgy, 41, 45
Slovak Learned Society, 71

INDEX

Slovak National Council, 88, 96
Slovak National Revival, 71, 81
Slovak People's Party, 82, 93
Slovak Volunteer Army, 88
Slovak Uprising of 1848 – 1849, 88 – 89
Slověne, 26
Slovenians, 26, 83
slovienčina, 26
Slovieni, 26, 31, 33, 45, 49
slovienska, 26
sloviensky, 26
Smútok, 82
Smrť Jánošíkova, 69
Sobieski, John, King of Poland, 63
Sokol, Ján, Archbishop-Metropolitan of Bratislava–Trnava, 104
Solúň, 35
Solúň Brothers, 35
Spiš, 94, 101
Spiš, Castle of, 58
Spišské Tomášovce, 25
Spytihnev, 47
Stephen I, King, 57
Stoličný Belehrad, 57, 60
Strečno, Castle of, 62
Sučany, 66
Sudetenland, 102
Suleiman I, Turkish Sultan, 63
Supljikač, Stevan, Ban of Serbia, 86
Svaroh, 18, 21
Svarožič, 18
Svätoboj, 45
Svätopluk I, King, 23, 36 – 37, 43, 45, 47, 54
Svätopluk II, Prince, 45, 47, 54
Svetovid, 18, 21
Szeged, 94
Šafárik, Pavol Jozef, 82 – 83
škriatok, 19
Štefánik, Milan Rastislav, Brigadier Gen., 95 – 96, 98
Štúr, Ľudovít, 69, 82, 84 – 85, 88
Štúrovo, 66
Šulek, Viliam, 86, 88
Šulekovo, 25, 86, 88

Tacitus, 18
Tatars, 59
Tatra Mountains, 17, 73, 75, 77
Terchová, 69

Theophylactus, 18
Theory of the Slovak Language, 82
Theodora, Byzantine Empress, wife of Justinian I, 48
Theodora, mother of Pope Pascal I, 42
Theotokos, 34
Thessalonian Brothers, 35, 41, 43, 90
Thessalonika, 30, 31, 35
Thessaloniki, 30
Thirty Years War, 65 – 66, 69
Thököly, Imre, 67
Tisa river, 17, 49
Tiso, Jozef Msgr., President of Slovakia, 97, 102
Tisza, Kalman, Hungarian Prime Minister, 90 – 91
Topoľčany, Castle of, 61
Torysa river, 50, 63
Trenčín, 27, 69
Trenčín, Castle of, 59 – 60
Triglav/Trihlav, 18
Trnava, 25, 104
Trniny, 25
Turčiansky Svätý Martin, 85, 89 – 90,
Turíce, 21
Turiec, 21, 57
Turkish invasion, 61, 63, 67
Turkish Terror, 66
Turks, 61, 63, 66 – 67, 86

Uhorsko, 49
Uhri/Ugri, 49
Uhrovec, 82
Ukraine, 17
Ukrainians, 83
United States of America, 100
Urban II, Pope, 57
Urban, Hungarian envoy, 61
Úroda, 19

Václav of Bohemia, King, 60
Váh river, 23, 27, 66
Vajanský, Svetozár Hurban, 82
Valentinian I, Roman Emperor, 17
Vallombrosian Benedictine Monks, 40
Vandals, 17
Varna, Battle of, 61
Vavrinec, 43
Velehrad, 41
Velleius Paterculus, 18
Veľká Bytča, 69

Veľká Mača, 25, 38
Velvet Revolution, 104
Venedae, 18
Verdun, Treaty of, 31
vedomkyne, 19
Venice, 39
Vesna, 19 – 20
veštice, 19
Via dei Querceti, 41
Via Labicana, 41
Via San Giovanni in Laterano, 41
Vienna, 47, 63, 66 – 67, 86, 88
Vienna, Battle of, 67
víla, 19
Világos, 89
Vindobona, 47
Virgin Mary, 33
Visigoths, 17
Vladislav, King of Poland, 61
vlkodlaci, 19
vodníci, 19
Vogastisburg, 27
Vogburg, 27
vojvoda, 21
Vosgate, Castle of, 27
Vratislav, Castle of, 47
Vyšehrad/Vyšegrad, 25, 60

Warsaw, 101
Warsaw Pact troops, 103 – 104
Wends, 18
Western High Tatra Mountains, 73, 75, 77
Westphalia, Peace of, 66
Wiching, 43
Wilhelm, 45
Windischgrätz, Prince Alfred, Austrian General, 86, 88
Wittenberg, Castle-church of, 63
World War I, 94 – 95
World War II, 102

Zagreb, 86
Zalavár, 25, 31
Zemplín, 25
Zmok, 19
Znachor, 19
žertva, 21
Žilina, 88
Živa, 19
žrec, 21